The Book of the Football Fanzines
Compiled by Phil Shaw

Preface

The proliferation of the fanzines and the emergence of the Football Supporters Association were virtually simultaneous. When the FSA was launched in August, 1985, our first attempt to found a Branch outside Merseyside took us to York where Frank Ormston of the seminal fanzine, *Terrace Talk*, invited us to hold a public meeting. Later that year, *Off the Ball* appeared for the first time, soon followed by *When Saturday Comes* and a variety of club-based publications which formed the first wave of fanzine success. Phil Shaw, then with *The Guardian*, played a part too for, without his regular publicising of the new arrivals as they emerged, many potential readers would never have known of their existence. (The FSA was also launched via a Letter to the Editor of the same paper — *The Guardian*'s got a lot to answer for!)

With sales of over 100,000 a month, the fanzines have succeeded for the first time in giving a true indication of the size of the 'alternative football network'. This growing band is also the natural base of the FSA's constituency — a huge body of football fans who want to do *more* than just jump up and down behind the goal. They have already convinced many people both inside and outside the game that they have a major role in football's future.

No wonder the established sports journalists are looking over their shoulders at the up-and-coming talents surfacing on the fanzine pages. When it comes to the *fine* detail of football supporting, the fanzine writers usually win hands down. Who else but a real Newcastle Utd fan (in *The Mag*) would spot that Mirandinha rolls his socks in the same way Jackie Milburn used to? Who else would realise the portentous significance of such a fact for their Cup run (unfortunately not entirely borne out . . .)?

For those readers unfamiliar with this new recipe for football writing, the following pages will be an exciting *hors d'oeuvres*; for confirmed fanzine addicts, a much valued 'action-replay'. I hope it will widen an already extensive audience and draw more football fans into *active* participation. The game certainly needs them like never before.

Rogan Taylor
FSA Chair

Foreword

I have but five autographs in my collection – those of two American musicians (Jimi Hendrix and Sam 'Lightnin' Hopkins) and three Scottish footballers (Bill Shankly, Billy Liddell and Kenny Dalglish). In a life thus pretty much dominated by football and pop music, I have admired those writers – and they have been depressingly few in number – who wrote either from the terraces or from the dance floor. In pop, far too many writers appear to have been motivated by the urge to demonstrate that, however emotionally damaged the stars they write about may be, they themselves are in a much worse state; in football, by an eagerness to join that happy circle where Jimmy Hill and Bobby Robson remember your first name. (It is one of my proudest boasts that I once refused to join a group being photographed with Bobby Robson).

At the end of the 1970s, and inflamed by punk rock, fans, bored with the strutting of the music weeklies, started generating their own magazines, recording their own often apparently unbalanced views with an exuberance that allowed no time for affectation. The first time I saw a similar approach brought to football was in the great Merseyside irregular, *The End*, an impudent farrago of music, football and social irresponsibility, rich in the atmosphere of the four ale bar.

Yet, despite *The End*, the sights and sounds witnessed in the Heysel Stadium kept me away from the match until the 1988-89 season, when not only *The Absolute Game*, *When Saturday Comes* and *Hit The Bar* but also *AWOL*, *When Sunday Comes* and *City Gent* encouraged me to watch Liverpool again and – perhaps more importantly – to join 50 others in observing Stowmarket hold Chatteris to a 1-1 draw in the Jewson Eastern Counties League.

The independent magazines have provided not only wild irreverence but also some of the most realistic pieces about Hillsborough, and the most persuasive arguments against such tomfoolery as the ID cards scheme and talk of Super Leagues. Whatever happens to football in the future, the fan has a voice – hundreds of voices – at last and can be heard not only in these pages but beyond, in the boardroom and even – if anyone is listening – in the Cabinet. That can only be for the good.

John Peel

It is a wet, windy Friday night on the terrracing – no, make that cinder-banking – exclusively reserved for away fans because it has no cover, no crash barriers, no tea bar, no toilets and no future except as the site for another Sainsbury's.

The tiny knot of visiting supporters, one deep, surges forward towards the six-foot high perimeter fencing as their team's left-winger breaks clear of the defence. He reaches the home penalty area, and squares a perfect pass inside to the unmarked No.9. Forty-six arms are raised in expectation... he can't miss...

Once the ball has been retrieved from what will shortly be the hypermarket's yoghurt section, the home side make the most of their escape. They score the only goal – off a knee, from what must have been an offside position, in time mysteriously added on by the referee.

A phalanx of local police escorts the away end to their coach, ignoring requests for the return of the umbrellas confiscated and making sure no one steps out of line on to the pavement, though not before all 3,783 home spectators are either in the pub or by the living-room fire.

The driver won't stop at the motorway café – which anyway has a sign saying 'No Football Coaches' – and 80 miles from home the bus splutters to a halt at the side of the road.

As the stoics shiver and wait for the AA, the team's luxury coach speeds past. The players seem to be cheerful enough, and an odd hand twitches and threatens a half-wave. The rural silence is shattered by a defiant chorus of 'We'll support you evermore', though the thought occurs to more than one that this time next year half that lot will probably be playing in the obtrusively sponsored pinstripes of the bunch who have just beaten them.

The team, as per manager's orders, is taking each match as it comes, and this one has gone. The board of directors are still in the hospitality suite sounding off about the yobs who aren't real supporters. The yobs, meanwhile, have paid for the privilege of getting the cold shoulder on the hard shoulder. All for the love of the game, *their* game.

THE FANZINE PHENOMENON

'Most players hate the fanzines. They tend to be critical of footballers and the way the game is run. Professional players are very wary of anything that makes fun of them – they can be absurdly loyal to the game's good image...

If the fanzines have a pet hate it's the ego-maniac in the boardroom. They hate the thought that a game which provokes the loyalty of a community should be run to suit the whims of a rich businessman.'
PAT NEVIN, Everton and Scotland winger.[1]

FOOTBALL is often called 'the People's Game', but the people who run it and indeed own its clubs are not the people invoked in that romantic, almost naive phrase.

The question of to whom the professional game 'belongs' has been asked as long as it has been played. A letter writer to the *Birmingham Mail* in 1892 said: 'I venture to suggest that the turn has come of the public who bring the grist to the mill. Why not covered accommodation for spectators, dry ground to stand on, and a reduced admission if possible? The profits will stand it. Many a wreath has been purchased by standing on wet ground on Saturday afternoons.'

Nearly a century on, the debate has been re-opened with fresh vigour, prompted by a sorry catalogue of disasters – in the literal sense, not as in

When Saturday Comes
The Half Decent FOOTBALL Magazine
June 1989 No. 28   50p

Hillsborough: Unanimous Verdict

It wasn't our fault

It wasn't our fault

Oh well, it must be our fault again

It wasn't our fault

*Sun*speak for an own goal – and debacles.

The tragedies at Bradford and Sheffield produced more than 150 wreaths. A Tory government obsessed with hooliganism set about imposing a compulsory membership scheme – in the face of opposition from clubs, police, fans and even some of its own MPs – while ignoring the less vote-worthy issue of spectator safety until it was too late.

The biggest clubs plotted to form a breakaway Super League, without any consultation of their supporters, out of vanity and greed.

Charlton suddenly abandoned The Valley for the alien turf of Crystal Palace's Selhurst Park (although there was to be a happy end to that saga). Tottenham sneered at their supporters, and at the local council, when they protested about the decision to build executive boxes on the popular-side 'Shelf' terracing. Spurs then called off the opening game of the 1988-89 season, because of building work, but not before fans had set out for White Hart Lane from all over the country.

In perhaps the most sinister development, Fulham and Queen's Park Rangers were to be merged at Shepherd's Bush, with 'yuppie' flats constructed at Craven Cottage, before public outcry embarrassed the property moguls into retreat. A similar threat hovers over Milltown, home of Ireland's most famous club, Shamrock Rovers of Dublin.

Aston Villa epitomised the store most clubs set by their

traditions when, in the cause of rampant commercialism, they abandoned their claret and blue shirts for a mélange of purple and pink that one reporter described as resembling a summer pudding.

In each instance – and these were the tip of a considerable iceberg – it was clear that the supporters who sustain football through thin and thinner were usually the last to be considered, let alone consulted.

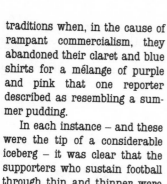

NOT THE VIEW
Celtic Fanzine   No. 8 50p

GET WELL SOON!

MALCONTENTS!

sing when we're fishing
No. 2 30p.

McGarvey Goes

INSIDE –
CUMMING – MAN OR MAMMAL?
IS RUGBY CRAP?
"OUR WAY TO WEMBLEY" ISSUE!

The SPUR
50p
NUMBER TWO   TEN SHILLIN'
Tottum are back, Tottum are back, ollé! ollé? Tottum are back, Tottum are back, ollé! ollé?

WELCOME BACK

All this happened at a time when executive-boxes, with their colour televisions and supply of Cabernet Sauvignon, were sprouting everywhere. When football's legendary 'missing millions' were being harangued by the Prime Minister and her Minister for Sport into believing they were bound to be attacked by vicious thugs if they gave the national game another go.

And when, as one sagacious peer put it in the House of Lords during a debate on Mr Moynihan's Football Spectators Bill, there was actually more chance of getting beaten up on the streets of Windsor or Bracknell than at a match.

The question of whose game it is has found resounding, positive answers. In the wake of the Heysel disturbances in which another 39 died in 1985, a militant pressure group was formed in Liverpool. The Football Supporters' Association (FSA) began to challenge the age-old perception of the fan as a passive, uncritical, gullible consumer with deep pockets who knew his/her place – which more often than not was on that wet, windy cinder-bank.

This radical upsurge needed a propagandist voice. It has found one in the subcultural and publishing phenomenon of the second half of the 1980s – the football fanzine. Late in 1989, there are around 200 such magazines. Most are club-based but there is a healthy sprinkling covering the game in general. Among the latter is *When Saturday Comes* (circulation 17,000 and rising – above the average gate for half the First Division), while the majority of teams in Britain have at least one publication devoted to them (Celtic's *Not The View*, with 11,000-plus sales per issue, is the market leader).

A survey of fanzines by the Sir Norman Chester Centre for Football Research, at Leicester University's Department of Sociology, found that the 'average circulation per issue of each fanzine ranged from 45 to 11,000, yet the majority (55 per cent) fell between 200 and 1,000 copies per issue'.

The researcher deduced from the findings this staggering statistic: 'When one calculates the number of issues per season and the average circulation per issue, then at a conservative estimate more than *one million* fanzines will be bought this season [1988-89].'

The message from virtually all these magazines, so varied in quality and allegiance, is clear. It is that football belongs not to television, to an elitist clutch of clubs, to rapacious agents or sensation-hungry tabloids, or to the shareholders and sponsors, but to the people whose pounds and partisanship sustain the sport. Fittingly, the FSA's own journal is called *Reclaim The Game*.

Your Favourite Over-Used Football Facts

It has occurred to us that some of the 'facts' in this award winning series are not, strictly speaking, facts at all, but oft-repeated cliches. All the same sort of nonsense, though, eh? This issue's selection includes contributions from Andy Oates and George Koussef. Teeth rotting prizes are on their way.

1. Duncan McKenzie could throw a golf ball the length of a football pitch.
2. The Birkenhead group Half-Man Half-Biscuit once recorded an amusing song called "All I Want For Xmas Is A Dukla Prague Away Kit"
3. George Best never played in the finals of a major tournament.
4. Kevin Moran is the only player to have been sent off in a Cup Final.
5. Wembley Stadium has changed hands yet again.
6. Tony Cottee repays a slice of that £2 million fee with another goal for Everton.
7. Southampton are the first league team this century to field three brothers in the same side.
8. Football fanzines are a *"phenomenon"*
9. Terry Venables is the only player to have represented England at every level.
10. Every non league side who reach the Third Round of the Cup are playing in *"their Cup Final"*

But how did it all start? The *Oxford English Dictionary*'s new, 20-volume edition (a snip at £1,500) traces the usage of the word 'fanzine' back to 1949 and the United States: 'A magazine for fans, especially science fiction.' After it was re-invented in Britain in the mid 1970s, the definition should have changed to 'for *and by* fans'. Anyone who attended a punk-rock or 'new-wave' gig at that time will remember having copies of *Ripped & Torn*, *Sniffin' Glue*, *48 Thrills*, *Temporary Hoarding* and other xeroxed paeans to the Sex Pistols, Clash, Damned, Jam *et al* thrust in their face.

Punk came in snarling and spitting at rock's establishment, many of them one-time rebels. The aim, apart from getting smashed, was to reclaim 'their' music from the giant record corporations and the over-produced, over-paid groups they perceived as having 'sold out'.

Time Out's rock editor felt sufficiently threatened to denounce punk as having 'the life expectancy of a scab'. It survived rather longer, but most of its central figures were soon incorporated into the mainstream by major labels. As Stuart Cosgrove, St Johnstone supporter and a

particularly perceptive music journalist, has pointed out: 'Not even at the glorious height of punk did fanzines come close to exposing the inner workings of the music industry – let alone incurring the wrath of the company boardrooms'.[2]

Cosgrove was alluding to reports that a number of clubs – from Tottenham, Arsenal, Celtic and Manchester United to Airdrie, Boston United and Wealdstone – had banned fanzines about them from their grounds. It has been remarked that punk changed nothing but the width of a generation's jeans; football fanzines, with their more campaigning approach, appear more capable of striking the relevant raw nerves and rallying support for genuine change.

There can be no denying, however, that this late 1980s publishing boom has taken more than its generic moniker from *Sniffin' Glue* and its ilk. By economic necessity, the felt-tip pen, typewriter, scissors and cow gum are still key production components, although several of the better-selling football fanzines have been able to go in for professional printing.

The links with the 'independent' music scene do not end there. John Peel, its DJ father-figure, regularly extols the virtues of Liverpool FC on his Radio 1 show; Pat Nevin, dubbed 'the first post-punk footballer' by the *New Musical Express* (and 'the first yuppie of football' by the *Chelsea Independent* fan-

zine!) told bemused tabloid hacks of his passion for groups like Crispy Ambulance and Joy Division; a Leeds band, The Wedding Present, called their debut LP 'George Best', and his picture rather than theirs adorned its sleeve; Half Man Half Biscuit, from Birkenhead, eulogised Tranmere Rovers in interviews and Subbuteo in song.

Scottish duo The Proclaimers sang of 'going to Kilmarnock to see Hibernian play', and a Hibs fanzine reciprocated by taking the title *The Proclaimer*. *Brian Moore's Head*, a Gillingham fanzine, produced a cover parodying the artwork for the Sex Pistols' 'Never Mind The Bollocks' album. Oxford's *Raging Bull* and West Ham's *On The Terraces* gave away flexi-disc pop singles.

And so on... even the titles *When Saturday Comes* and *The Absolute Game* (a magazine covering Scottish football in general) were taken from songs by The Undertones and The Skids respectively.

Tim Colliew of the specialist London bookshop Sportspages, pointing out that several football-fanzine editors actually started out with punk publications, said: 'It's a fairly natural association. Most are put out by lads under the age of 25 and the most important things in their lives are music and football.'[3]

Yet there was an earlier, seminal influence. *Foul* – the name was a deliberate parody of magazines like *Shoot!* and *Goal* – first appeared in October 1972; its 34th and last issue hit the newsstands exactly four years later. Issues 1-9 were typewritten; from No.10 onwards it was typeset and distributed by the

firm who handled *Private Eye*.

Concerned with the game as a whole rather than any particular club, *Foul* kicked against the frightening and frightened football of Revie and Ramsey; against reactionary administrators, like the late Football League secretary Alan Hardaker (incidentally, there is a current fanzine called *Hardaker Rides Again . . .*); and against ego-maniac managers.

As Mike Ticher, founder of the *Foul*-influenced *When Saturday Comes*, put it: 'It railed against the whole structure of football and often did fine investigative jobs on individual clubs and their masters. Most importantly, it was very funny.'[4]

'Football's alternative paper', as it styled itself, *Foul* was edited by a group of Cambridge graduates, only one of whom, Steve Tongue, has made a career out of football writing; most of today's fanzine editors have been to Cambridge only to watch Fourth Division or Southern League football. It may have failed to bring down the FA or force Norman Hunter to hang up his studs, but *Foul* did open its pages to the 'ordinary' fan. And its *Private Eye*-style format (the 'rag-outs' of newspaper gaffes, the spoof tabloid letters, the cartoons and 'bubble' cap-

tions on photos) left a blueprint for the next generation.

The *bêtes-noires* have changed in the ensuing decade; for Ramsey, Hardaker, Hunter and Leeds read Robson, Maxwell, Souness and Wimbledon (although Brian Clough is still around and more, er, idiosyncratic than ever, while the combination of Vinny Jones and Leeds was a real throwback). And where *Foul* was concerned with exposing foot-up hackers and supine hacks, the 1980s fanzines have had to confront the sport in its post-Heysel, post-Maxwell state and to tackle fundamental issues such as misconceptions about the extent of hooliganism (labelled 'the British disease' by lazy journalists), the conniving of chairmen and property developers, and scheming between TV moguls and self-styled Super Leaguers.

THE "CITY GENT"
SUPPORTERS' NEWS
PUBLICATION OF CITY TRAVEL CLUB'TS (BCD)

1st EDITION
NOVEMBER
·1984·

20 pence

CONTENTS: CES PODD'S LIFE WITHOUT CITY...
TREVOR CHERRY SPEAKS....a frank interview
What the Bantam Saw...the latest hot gossip
THE ALAN WOOD TEMPERANCE SERMON...CAMRA Guide
Plus much more...

The first club-oriented fanzines – *Terrace Talk* (York City), *City Gent* (Bradford City), *The Web* (Queen's Park), *Pink 'n' Blue Bushwacker* (Dulwich Hamlet) and *Fingerpost* (West Bromwich Albion) – had no single battle to fight. But their emergence, after two decades in which football fans had become media folk devils, helped in a greater cause: that of restoring the dignity of the game's followers.

Many of those who started the early fanzines had grown up as readers of *Shoot!* and *Match*, colour magazines for children and adolescents which tend to gloss over the unsavoury aspects of football. Team photos and ghosted personality columns are their staple diet; criticism rarely rears its head.

The case of Gordon Strachan's transfer from Manchester United to Leeds in March 1989 offers a classic example of the puerile approach of such magazines. Strachan chose a Second Division club in preference to two in the First, but there was no mystery as to how he had arrived at his decision. Ron Atkinson, who had hoped to buy him for Sheffield Wednesday, announced ruefully: 'There was no way we could match what Leeds were offering.'

Strachan, understandably for a professional in the later stages of his career, had taken the best offer available. *Shoot!*, meanwhile, asked its readers to believe that 'Wanted man Gordon Strachan declared his passion for Leeds almost before the ink had dried on his £300,000 deadline-busting deal.' The player was pictured in the now-obligatory pose with club scarf, and neither the word 'money' nor its usual stand-in 'personal terms' was mentioned in the accompanying 300-word piece.

For the discerning fan who is disinclined, in the words of a million fathers (including my own) to 'grow out of this football thing' but who nevertheless does not want to be patronised, there is a problem of what to read. Magazines aimed at the older end of the market, such as *Football Monthly*, tend to ape their junior brethren by perpetuating euphemisms like tough-tackling (dirty) or want-away (greedy).

One of its colour competitors, *Football Today*, at least appears to be facing up to issues such as Mr Moynihan's Football Spectators Bill. The magazine handed out thousands of red cards for spectators to brandish at the Tannoy announcer's behest during a televised match between Aston Villa and Manchester United, and its cover bears the street-cred slogan 'Endorsed by the PFA'. But the format, tone and style remain basically old-fashioned, and it is certainly no *When Saturday Comes*.

In short, with the possible exception of promising, fanzine-influenced Scottish newcomer *The Punter*, none of the magazines available in the big retailers demonstrates much sympathy for the way the game is perceived by a significant portion of its audience. They do not appreciate football's place within a broader cultural context, nor understand the football-match experience. They appear, to put it generously, to be out of touch.

That 'experience' often includes having a convivial drink before a game with 'rival' supporters, and exchanging anecdotes and information about police/press/players/programmes/pies and pints. Journals like Bradford's *City Gent* and *The Pie* (Notts County) often fill several pages with details of where to find the best-kept beer or a good curry on away trips. Although *City Gent* adopted the slogan 'The Voice of Bantam Progressivism' and lists among its contributors the militant Labour MP Pat Wall, it sometimes seems closer to *Suppin' Ale* than *Sniffin' Glue*.

The most striking characteristic of *City Gent* is the warmth and concern (summed up by John Dewhirst, one of its editorial team, as 'critical allegiance') its contributors show towards the Bradford club and the game in general. They were quick to produce a 'special' in aid of the Hillsborough Disaster Fund. Unusually, City's

players, directors and staff have cooperated with the *Gent*, whose founders prefer to call it an 'independent supporters magazine' rather than a fanzine.

City Gent was typical of the first wave of publications (No.1 came in October 1984) in its attempts at bridge-building between supposedly antagonistic followers of different teams. They drew the line at Leeds United (perhaps understandably, in view of a chip-van blaze started by Leeds 'supporters' at City's temporary home, Odsal

Stadium, 18 months after the Valley Parade tragedy) and published a provocative booklet sarcastically titled *Leeds United – The Glory Years*, in which every page was blank.

Generally, though, differences were played down and, with the burgeoning FSA playing the leading role, common grievances and shared aspirations magnified.

Off the Ball's arrival in January 1986 – seven months after Brussels and Bradford – marked a significant advance. A national magazine, which was its greatest strength and its main weakness, the highlight of the first issue was a feature based on interviews with Wolves' chief executive and the chairman of the then-outlawed supporters'

club. (This was pre-Graham Turner and Steve Bull, when Wolves were rapidly sliding down the divisions under dubious ownership.) The writer, Adrian Goldberg, concluded that what remained of the Molineux faithful must 'get radical'.

I was writing *The Guardian*'s 'Soccer Diary' at the time and chose to lead the column with a piece welcoming *Off the Ball*, beginning: 'Libel lawyers are not the only ones who miss *Foul*...' I may have been over-anxious to recreate my youth by implying there was a qualitative similarity; in truth the first edition was short of good writing, humour and design awareness. But it was a start.

My concluding remark that 'its grey pages contrast starkly with the vitality of rock fanzines' appeared to have been taken to heart, for in the following two years *Off the Ball* came up with a series of classic covers. The best, for the October/November 1987 issue, grafted Graeme Souness's head on to Michael Jackson's androgynous leather persona. The collage made a 'satirical comment on Souness's psychopathic hardman image' according to Stuart Cosgrove.

Another cover, of which *Foul* would have been proud, was headlined 'Salute to Portsmouth' and highlighted the First Division newcomers' staggering litany of indiscipline and even crime. A third depicted the acquisitive millionaire publisher Robert Maxwell, who, remember, had tried to commit merger most foul by uniting Reading and Oxford as 'Thames Valley Royals', only to back down in the face of opposition he condemned as 'parochial' and 'conservative'. Blood was dripping from his mouth, in a pastiche movie poster for 'Mad Max 4'. 'Now showing at Derby, Oxford, Reading and Watford', it said, listing clubs in whom Maxwell had an interest or was, as it were, showing an interest. It added portentously: 'At a ground near you soon'.

Although, like *Foul*, *Off the Ball*'s quality tended to be uneven precisely because it offered a forum for anyone who cared to put pen to paper, former *Foul* contributor/TV scriptwriter Stan Hey was sufficiently impressed by its early progress to call it 'the most radical voice' and praise its 'amusing distaste for local (Midlands) chairmen'.[5]

In March, 1986, *When Saturday Comes* arrived, as an offshoot of a music fanzine named *Snipe!*. Mike Ticher, having apparently written, laid out and typed most of the first issue, set out its editorial policy on the front. Ticher, a Chelsea supporter for whom Pat Nevin personified good and Ken Bates evil, was stronger on what his publication would not be about than on what it aimed to achieve.

'It's not going to be clichéd, hackneyed, lazy journalism', he wrote. 'It's not going to be banal, ghostwritten platitudes. It's not going to be tedious, whitewashing interviews, it's not going to be full of statistics or match reports, and it's certainly not going to indulge in petty rivalries ... All that stuff is available in abundance elsewhere.

'What it might be a bit more like is the sort of thing you talk about in the pub. Gossip, stories, arguments, some serious things that never get discussed anywhere else, like racism at football but mostly not.'

If that sounded sanctimonious – a common fanzine failing, often accompanied by blanket dismissiveness about 'the media' or attacks on 'the so-called Minister for Sport' à la *Private Eye*'s revolutionary student columnist 'Dave Spart' – Ticher redeemed himself with a leavening of wit. 'What is it about certain clubs (e.g. Liverpool, Ipswich, Arsenal),' he asked, 'that attracts so many players with big noses? Does anyone in football actually *like* Ron Saunders?

'These are the sort of questions I've always wanted the answers to, but no publication ever tells me. Maybe *When Saturday Comes* will: it's up to you.'

The response was such that Ticher and his collaborator Andy Lyons were soon producing professionally printed, stylishly laid-out issues. A strong editorial line had been established in No.1's attack on the ever-changing team strips ('Come on you blue two-tone hoops with red and white trim and a little emblem on the sleeve and the manufacturers' logo and the

sponsors' name across the chest'), and many of the readers who contributed as *When Saturday Comes* became the best-seller showed a strong empathy and considerable journalistic flair.

Some of them, suitably stimulated, invested in scissors, paste and Letraset and set to work on fanzines about their own clubs. Mike Wilson, writing in *The Observer*, reckoned *When Saturday Comes* and others had 'won legitimacy for fanzines'.[6]

They certainly provided an inspirational example, though legitimacy is unlikely to be high on many lists of editorial priorities, particularly among those who may regard themselves as punk's progeny. Some of the titles speak volumes for their subversive aims: e.g. *Not The View* (an obvious dig at *The Celtic View*, the Glasgow club's tame official newspaper); *Kick Up The R's* (run by Queen's Park Rangers fans who see no contradiction in combining partisanship with the need to kick boardroom backsides); *Tired and Weary* (pointedly plucked by long-suffering Birmingham City supporters from the terrace anthem 'Keep Right On to the End of the Road'); and *Chelsea Independent* (a name clearly intended to distance its publishers, the Independent Supporters' Association, from the more acquiescent official supporters' organisation and from the chairman Ken Bates).

Then there are the hard-nosed realists (pessimists), like *The Final Hurdle* (invented by Dundee United fans because, presumably, their team keeps falling at it); Brighton's *And Smith Must Score!* which commemorates the painful moment in which Gordon Smith missed a chance from which Cyril Smith would have expected to score, and the FA Cup slipped from their grasp; *Elm Park Disease*, from Reading, which is self-explanatory; and *NHS*, produced by stalwarts of homeless Vauxhall-Opel Leaguers Kingstonian, which stood for No Home Stadium, although the club has now put down new roots at nearby Norbiton.

There are those which draw on the terrace songs and chants: they include my own favourite, the brilliantly titled *Sing When We're Fishing* (Grimsby Town), which works on a number of levels; *One-Nil Down, Two-One Up* (derived from Arsenal's gloating chant about famous recoveries against Spurs and Liverpool); *There's Only One F in Fulham* (geddit?); *One Team in Ulster* and *Follow, Follow* (lifted from the Loyalist – that's with a capital 'L' – songs of the fans of Linfield and Rangers respectively).

Some simply reflect gushing adulation, notably *Brian* (Clough, of course), *King of the Kippax* (after Manchester City's popular side, Kippax Street), and *Flashing Blade* (Sheffield United, nicknamed the Blades).

Other names aim to make a point, like *Marching Altogether* (by Leeds Fans United Against Racism and Fascism) and *From Behind Your Fences* (Boston), which was given a terrible new relevance by Hillsborough; a few come across like applications for a sub-editor's job on *The Guardian*, with punning titles like *Leyton Orientear*, *Abbey Rabbit* (Cambridge United), and *Witton Wisdom* (Aston Villa).

One or two show real wit and imagination, such as *When Sunday Comes* (a Liverpool fanzine's subtle way of pointing out how often their team were selected for ITV's live Sunday show 'The Match'), *The Memoirs of Seth Bottomley* (Port Vale – named after an imaginary ex-player created to humour moaning older Valeites, one of whom, the editor swears, was heard to remark that a present-day midfielder

'couldner owd a candle ter Bottomley'), and *Champion Hill Street Blues* (Dulwich – one of a number of high-quality efforts by non-League followers remarkable for circulations often higher than the team's average crowd).

Others are unashamedly, self-consciously wacky, especially *Brian Moore's Head*, taken from a Half Man Half Biscuit song in honour of the balding ITV commentator and former Gillingham director which originally had the suffix *Looks Uncannily Like The London Planetarium*, Middlesbrough's *Fly Me To The Moon*, Cardiff's *Intifada* (Arabic for 'uprising'), and St Johnstone's *Wendy Who?* (as in 'Oh Wendy Saints go marching in . . .').

Stan Hey, a former *Foul*-mouth, detected 'a commendable sense of fraternity and mutual promotion between all the magazines, as they have realised from the onset that they share common enemies'.[7] In September 1988, there was the sight of Leeds *and* Chelsea supporters joining forces before a match between ostensibly sworn enemies to picket and leaflet Elland Road in the cause of anti-racism.

That magnanimity is not universal, particularly among Scottish fanzines, although the owner of the Edinburgh shop Football Crazy, Alan Cunningham, has spotted 'a lot of cross-loyalties where a fan of one team will buy another club's fanzines'.

For instance, Rangers' *Follow, Follow* called Celtic the 'athletic wing of the IRA' and can not apparently see the contradiction in attacking the barracking of black players and poking fun at the supposed stupidity of their rivals' Irish Catholic supporters, whom they refer to as 'beggars'. Dundee's *Derry Rumba*, a title with sectarian conotations, depicted Dundee United's black striker Raphael Meade with a bone through his nose. *Heartbeat*, produced by Lancashire-based Heart of Midlothian stalwarts, was let down in its debut issue by schoolboy jokes at Hibernian's expense.

In most magazines, fans have found funnier, almost affectionate ways of expressing traditional antagonisms than saying merely 'We hate the bastards in red/

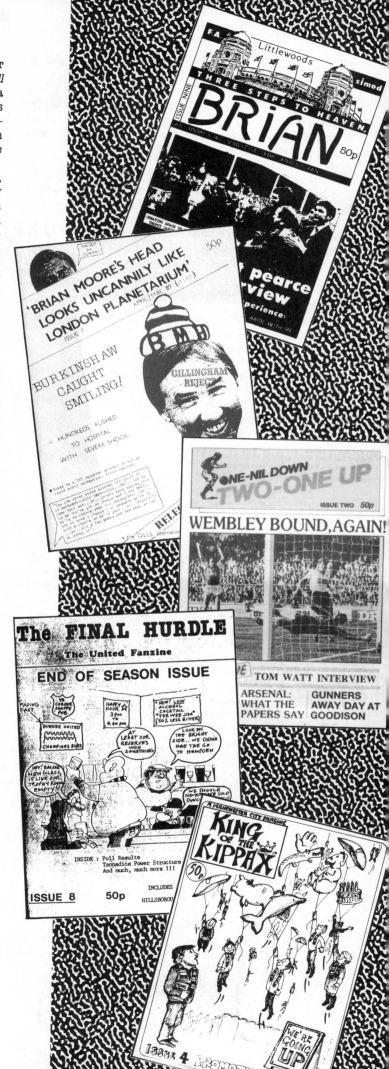

blue/green'. Witness the series run in both *Flashing Blade* and Chesterfield's *Crooked Spireite* entitled 'They Refused To Play For Wednesday'; or the balloon bearing a picture of the Dunfermline manager Jim Leishman given away in the *Falkirk Unofficial Fanzine*, whose editors considered him to be just that — to use the vernacular, a big balloon.

Indeed, the Falkirk publication epitomises those produced by fans of the middle tier of Scottish clubs, like Kilmarnock, Raith Rovers and Airdrie, which tend to convey greater wit and passion than fanzines devoted to the bigger clubs.

That sense of humour, allied to a cutting edge, is an essential ingredient in the better fanzines. *Brian* ran a series on players' hairstyles alongside critiques of poor facilities at grounds. *Not The View* dealt with the subject of racism in Scottish football and offered a more acceptable object of ridicule, the Rangers player-manager. Taking the Proclaimers' hit song 'Letter From America', it produced a new lyric: 'If you go will you send back/Souness to Sampdoria/Take a look at your full-backs/Two million for absolute crap'. *The Spur* campaigned against ID cards while having fun with Tony Adams's obsession with claiming offside decisions for Arsenal.

Self-mockery is an element in many fanzines. *The Spur* adapted Paul Gascoigne's nickname 'Gazza' to 'Guzzler' in recognition of his eating prowess, and several run 'Best & Worst XI' sections. *When Skies Are Grey* celebrates some of Everton's more embarrassing signings in 'They Gave Us The Blues', *Not The View* has a feature called 'They Embarrassed The Hoops', and *Killie Ken* remembers the 'Chocolate Teapots' (as in 'he's as much use as a . . .') of Kilmarnock.

It is true that many fanzine 'attacks' walk a fine line between irreverence and name-calling. But in the context of the dominant football press — the tabloids' fantasy world of 'now-I-must-tell-all' revelations, verbal sniping, plus fiction masquerading as transfer news, and the sometimes po-faced or pretentious posturing of the broadsheets — they perform the function of a disarmingly blunt antidote.

'Alternative' media are invariably preoccupied with their 'establishment' contemporaries. *Foul* ran some memorable spoofs, of the *Sun*'s shock-horror-probe headline style and of a 'Brian Glanville' report from The Den . . . in Italian. Tabloid pastiches are perhaps overworked in today's fanzines, but *Glenmalure Gazzette* (Shamrock Rovers) shows that the 'serious' press is still fair game by lampooning a certain controversial pundit as 'Eamon Grumpy'.

The fanzines also help to demystify the notion that 'fans' and 'writers' are, of necessity, breeds apart. (Scottish football journalists, as one of their number noted, are merely fans with typewriters.) There is real merit in many of the contributions herein, though in most cases their authors have neither journalistic training nor experience.

Meanwhile, the fanzine phenomenon shows no sign of burning out. (Its status as such was confirmed in *When Saturday Comes* 'Your Favourite Over-Used Football Facts' section; alongside 'The Cup is a great leveller' and 'John Barnes never turns it on for England', it told us 'Football fanzines are a phenomenon'.) It has even spread to Italy, where *giornali del tifo* have begun to appear.

The bug has bitten other sports, too, and by the Spring of 1989 four Rugby League fanzines were on sale — *The Steam Pig* (Bradford Northern), *Flag Edge Touch* (Hull KR), *The Tangerine Dream* (Chorley Borough) and *The Loiner* (Leeds). The first-named gained instant kudos when the Bradford board banned it from being sold inside their (council-owned) Odsal Stadium.

There is also a self-styled 'alternative' cricket journal, *Sticky Wicket*, which has a full-colour cover and slick design. Rugby Union, as yet, has no fanzines, unless one counts the *Daily Telegraph*.

Andy Lyons, who took over as editor of *When Saturday Comes* when Mike Ticher responded to Chelsea's relegation in 1988 by going to live in Australia, said during the build-up to 1989-90 that he was hearing of new titles each day. His magazine (which curiously never calls itself a 'fanzine') has a full-time staff of four and a word-processor. It has even begun to appear on the shelves of W.H. Smith. So much for street credibility!

When Saturday Comes also demonstrates a marketing awareness which belies its bedsit origins and will probably ensure its survival after some of its rivals and offspring have folded.

It sells T-shirts bearing the magazine's masthead and slogan ('The Half Decent Football Magazine'), produces polished advertising inserts for subscription offers, and organised a trip to watch England in Albania which took the product's name into millions of homes via TV, radio and the press.

Lauded in the quality dailies, doubtless to murmurs of 'sell out' from some provincial scissors-and-paste iconoclasts, it is one of the exceptions to the rule. For every neat, new-tech publication facilitated by the advent of cheap-ish 'desk-top' publishing, like the outstanding *An Imperfect Match* (Arsenal/European football) and *Fortune's Always Hiding* (West Ham), or, from the other end of the football spectrum, Kidderminster's impressive *The Soup*, there are two or three distinctly home-made efforts.

But where do the fanzines go from here? Heading 'upmarket' takes time, money and contacts, so that may not be a viable option for many editors even if they wanted so to do. Most are labours of love anyway, making little or no profit. Those produced by individuals may fall by the wayside as enthusiasm wanes or ideas dry up. Those which involve disparate talents, like the *City Gent*, will surely evolve and, dare one say it, become established.

It may be that saturation point will be reached, both in terms of numbers of publications available and the size of the buying public, after which there would have to be a degree of rationalisation.

It is conceivable that regional-rather than club-based fanzines could prosper. The potential audience would, of course, be greater than for productions restricted to one team, although against that must be set the possibility that the inevitable watering down of partisanship might make joint efforts bland.

The success or otherwise of *400 Yards* (Notts County and Nottingham Forest) will be fascinating to observe. Such a format looks a more plausible way forward than the fanzine devoted to two unconnected clubs, of which *UTD United* (West Ham and Dundee United) was an unexpected trailblazer. Incidentally, by issue 2 the latter's co-editors had not even met!

Merger of a different kind would make more sense where more than one fanzine is produced for one club – e.g. Arsenal, Cardiff and Hibernian (four each), West Ham and Charlton (three apiece), or, down the scale, Northwich Victoria (two).

Another possible trend is towards fanzines produced for specific matches, where they can be sold on the terraces, almost as surrogate programmes. *The Memoirs of Seth Bottomley* was shrewdly launched the day Port Vale played host to Wolves before their biggest crowd in a quarter-century. It sent up the phony 'welcome to our visitors' platitudes found in most programmes: 'We thank you for your cash but hope you go home miserable after a good hiding.' There was also a programme-style profile of Steve Bull. *Seth's* local rival, *The Oatcake*, is produced for every Stoke City home fixture.

City Gent was actually started because of dissatisfaction with the club programme. One cannot help feeling that Bradford City, among others, should now do the decent thing and hand over to their erudite followers. City have made an enlightened start by giving the *Gent*'s editor, Mick Dickinson, a page in the programme in which he plugs fanzines, fraternity and the FSA. How long before the first 'official match-day fanzine'?

A more interesting possibility is that fanzines will evolve into broad-based 'lifestyle' journals taking in music, film, books and other facets of popular culture. *AWOL*, produced by Meadowbank Thistle followers, has built a circulation around twice the club's average gate of 750 with a polished product bristling with record, gig and movie reviews plus pieces on nuclear power and fox-hunting – alongside swipes at Stenhousemuir and Stranraer. It has become essential reading for Edinburgh's renaissance persons, as has *Hull, Hell and Happiness* (Hull City) on north Humberside with a similar cocktail.

AWOL's cartoons are of a particularly high standard, as are those in *Bernard of the Bantams*, an offshoot of *City Gent*. The success of *Viz* suggests there may be a sizeable potential readership for a less parochial football-cartoon magazine.

Talk of music brings us full circle. If the 1970s punk fanzines changed little, as Stuart Cosgrove claims, what will historians make of their football successors?

They will record rightly, that their contribution to punctuation, literacy and the laws of libel was often roughly on a par with Paul Channon's to transport or Mike Channon's to grammar (the latter's gormless TV catchphrase from 1986 is now immortalised in the humour-fanzine *The Lad Done Brilliant*).

They will also note, one trusts, that along with the craze for inflatables – notably bananas, rainbow trout posing as haddock, pink panthers and black puddings – fanzines contributed much towards the game's greater sense of fun and tolerance between the nadir of 1985 and the numbing *déjà vu* of Hillsborough four years later.

If that were to be their legacy, it would be enough. But there is evidence to suggest that football's new wave really do have the clout to agitate successfully for change. *The Spur* was in the vanguard of a campaign by a group of Tottenham supporters (working under the acronym LOTS – Left On The Shelf) to stop their club, or rather their plc, from destroying the most popular

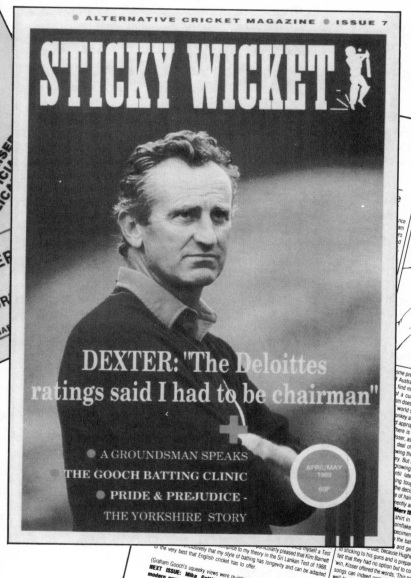

● ALTERNATIVE CRICKET MAGAZINE ● ISSUE 7

STICKY WICKET

DEXTER: "The Deloittes ratings said I had to be chairman"

APRIL/MAY 1989
60P

● A GROUNDSMAN SPEAKS
● THE GOOCH BATTING CLINIC
● PRIDE & PREJUDICE – THE YORKSHIRE STORY

Meda££ion MAN

...me pressure from a mountainous assault of mail. H K More has nominated Australian paceman **Merv Hughes** as Medallion Man of the Month. It ...find more contrasting characters than H K and the man who has become ...of a culturally deficient nation for his bizarre on-field antics, but then ...sm does have a habit of breaking down barriers amongst the more geekish ...world society. How, you may wonder, can a man whose fielding is akin ...onkey and whose batting scarcely allows willow on to be laid on leather, ...d appropriate as a winner of this prestigious competition. If this is not ...here is his bowling. Apart from one rather fortuitous display against ...sser, as **Hughes** is known to the more perceptive watchers of cricket, ...deal of time turning towards the pickets where some sympathetic ...wing the ball back to the nearest fielder, whose duty it is to retrieve ...ry. But back to the reasons why Kisser won this prestigious award ...growing number of other challengers. **Hughes** has a large walrus ...until late 1988 sported an uncontrollable thatch of wavy hair. ...ing tough might improve his lamentable performances in Test ...the decision to have a crew-cut whilst retaining his absurd facial ...e of hairstyle or not, this devotee of medallionism kept a rather ...ently around his neck and as he curves into bowl, like an out ...**Merv the Swerve** has been seen to even undo another button ...shirt in order to give his medallion (which he got free from ...cornflakes packet) maximum movement. It therefore bounces ...specimen's heaving chest as he delivers, which apparently ...p the batsman a little bit more than his liberal distribution ...and general crap could ever do on their own. But credit ...club, because Hughes has commendable tunnel vision when it comes ...o sticking to his guns and is prepared to go out on a limb to look stupid, the judges ...win, Kisser offered the words, 'This proves that lovers of treacley country and western ...songs can indeed compete at all levels of the fashion league'. SW readers will do ...well to avoid Hughes off the field this summer, as he is known to sport a fetching ...range of gaudy shirts and flared trousers which may or may not have been worn ...by members of Sweet in the mid 1970's. Additionally he has been seen to thrive ...on congratulating members of his own team, following the dismissal of one of the ...opposition, with something approaching passion, hence his rather obvious nick- ...name.

...lusively that my style of batting has longevity and can be adapted ...to the very best that English cricket has to offer.

(Graham Gooch's squeeky views were re-interpreted by none other than Alan Lee)

NEXT ISSUE: Mike Gatting advises on fielding short-leg in the modern game

...ed myself a Test ...particularly pleased with my theory in the Sri Lankan Test of 1988 ...felt that they had no option but to confer MoM on him. When told of his prestigious

STICKY WICKET 11

stretch of terracing at White Hart Lane. In March 1989, Tottenham unexpectedly announced concessions which would allow 3,000 supporters to continue to stand on The Shelf. 'Big deal' was a common reaction, but the decision represented a change of heart out of keeping with the club's previous contemptous attitude.

Later the same day, a packed meeting of Charlton fans heard that after 3½ years' exile at Crystal Palace, their team would soon be going back to the Valley. Lennie Lawrence, the Charlton manager, praised the campaigners' tenacity in classic managerial parlance – 'They got a result' – but perhaps more significantly, the journalist Patrick Collins highlighted the role of 'an excellent alternative magazine [*Voice of the Valley*] dedicated to a return'. Praise indeed from that bastion of 'alternative' values, *The Mail on Sunday*.[8]

It would be facile to suggest, for instance, that Irving Scholar said to his directors: 'Right – *The Spur* has got us by the short and curlies... what are we going to offer them?' But the very fact that several top clubs have banned and harrassed fanzine-sellers suggests they are aware of the thorn in their sides, and, by implication, of their views. The Leicester University survey found that 34 per cent of fanzine editors described their club's attitude as 'opposed'.

As the 1988-89 season closed amid sadness and anger at the deaths of more 'ordinary supporters' – and optimistically, implicit recognition by Lord Justice Taylor's Hillsborough inquiry that spectators actually have rights when he gave the FSA equal representation with the FA, clubs and police – it was clear that the fanzine's capacity to get up the appropriate noses was undiminished.

It was not just the big clubs. Grimsby Town officials alerted police to the fact that 'bogus programmes' were being sold (it was *Sing When We're Fishing*); one seller was arrested and detained for 20 minutes while officers muttered about prosecution under the Obscene Publications Act.

And at one leading non-league club, fanzine attacks on the sale of players prompted a rapid response. The editor was instantly banned from the stadium and, he told *The Independent's* 'Sports Diary', informed that he would be 'buried in the ground' and phoned at home when what he describes as 'totally inaccurate allegations about my sexuality' were made! Clearly, the fanzines must be doing something right...

Three years after I used *The Guardian's* 'Soccer Diary' to welcome *Off the Ball*, one of my successors on the column, Stephen Bierley, felt moved to write: 'Fanzines have been one of the delights of football in the past few years, glorious pulsating beacons of irreverence, wit and real information.'[9]

What they prove is that there are people who love the game and see its funny side (and I don't mean the BBC dredging up 'comedian' Stan Boardman every time Liverpool reach Wembley); who are naive enough to believe the clubs in whom they invest emotionally and financially belong to them, and criticise only because they care; who would not sit in an executive-box if they were paid to, because they value the sense of togetherness they feel on the terraces and would not be able to sing their hearts out 'for the lads' behind double glazing; who do not ambush rival fans except with offers of a pint, or make 'monkey' grunts at black players.

If that sounds like you, read on. Better still, write on. If you are wondering when your club will be getting a fanzine, maybe you are missing the point.

Football fanzines are an idea whose time has come. Whose game is it anyway?

REFERENCES
1 Stuart Cosgrove, 'Off the ball, off the wall', in City Limits, 17-24 March 1988.
2 Ibid.
3 Quoted in Lloyd Bradley, 'A right result', Q Magazine, March 1988.
4 Mike Ticher, Foul!: Best of Football's Alternative Paper 1972-76, Sportspages/Simon & Schuster, 1987.
5 Stan Hey, 'Fanfare for the common supporter', The Independent, 18 December 1987.
6 Mike Wilson, 'Putting the boot in from the terraces', The Observer, 8 January 1989.
7 Stan Hey, ibid.
8 Patrick Collins, 'The real identity', Mail on Sunday, 26 March 1989.
9 Stephen Bierley, 'Mad about the Mariners', The Guardian, 18 February 1989.

FF THE BALL

ISSUE 10 AUGUST/SEPTEMBER 1987 — 40p

SALUTE TO PORTSMOUTH

VINCE HILAIRE
4 BOOKINGS
1 SENDING OFF

KENNY SWAIN
3 BOOKINGS

ALAN KNIGHT
(GOALIE)
3 BOOKINGS

MICK TAIT
6 BOOKINGS
1 SENDING OFF
1 DISPUTE CHARGE
(£250 FINE)

PAUL HARDYMAN
10 BOOKINGS
1 SENDING OFF

MICK THOMAS
1 BOOKING

KEVIN O'CALLAGHAN
3 BOOKINGS

EAMON COLLINS
1 BOOKING

MICK KENNEDY
8 BOOKINGS
1 SENDING OFF
1 DISREPUTE CHARGE
(£5,000 FINE)

PAUL WOOD
1 BOOKING

NOEL BLAKE
4 BOOKINGS

BILLY GILBERT
5 BOOKINGS
1 SENDING OFF
1 DISREPUTE CHARGE
(£350 FINE)

KEVIN DILLON
3 BOOKINGS
1 SENDING OFF

MICK QUINN
9 BOOKINGS
1 JAIL SENTENCE

KEVIN BALL
2 BOOKINGS

DIVISION ONE HERE THEY COME
CLUB HONOURS 1986/1987

* 6 Sendings Off
* 64 Bookings
* 1 Player Jailed
* 2 Players Arrested at the Ground
* 3 Players Sent Off in One Match

* 3 Players Charged with Disrepute
* Goalkeeper Booked 3 Times
* £2,250 Fine plus £2,000 Suspended from F.A. over Disiplinary Record
* £1,000 Fines for Illegal Club

LIVERPOOL
WAL
PRESTO
BOLTO

St. Annes who might consider our offer a touch ... that the League are prepared to look a gift horse ... finances are in such a parlous state ... decision to withdraw from their sponsorship of ... reconsider.

YOU'RE WINNING

above the level of 'The Sun' back page risks a
... ctively invites it, subtitling Sing When You're
... filling its pages with generous references to
... as if to let us know where he's at, maan.
... tyle" is a genuinely thought provoking book
... rayed in the media, the rise of
... as football's last Golden Age of innocence is
... and tactics, he insists, were present then as
... ever since it became professional. What was
... knew their place, and the pundits are really
... following abolition of the maximum wage,
... to the past in the modern world, football,

When Saturday Comes

August 1988 — No. 18 — 40p

England Name Robson Successor

INSIDE

Football League: Behind Closed Doo...

Self-Indulgence Spec...

Letters

Please note that all correspondence will be considered for the letters page unless it specifically states otherwise.

Dear WSC

I thought I should bring to the attention of all fans of clubs outside the biggest five, a snippet of irony from Manchester United fans after their absolute outclassing by AC Milan in the recent, as billed, European challenge match.

The usual fair-minded, objective, unbiased, non-sectarian, lovers-of-the-game-in-general United fans were jumping to the defence of their team. *"It's not fair"* went up the cry. Rather than analyse the weakness of the domestic league over the last few seasons, their rationale was that *"it's not fair that these rich European teams can buy up all the best players like Gullit for £5m".*

What a change of fortunes for a mega loadsamoney club to be on the receiving end. Maybe they will spare a thought next game for the Burnleys, Coventrys and

Middlesbroughs of the game after Fer... out Martin Edwards' cheque book th... summer.

David Curtis,
Manchester.

* Then again, maybe they won't.

Dear WSC

The prices of food, clothes, el... (including players!) go up. An... days you'll have to raise the ... Last season, the directors c... loss at Fulham, and just n... out thousands to improve ... new boilers etc.

The increase in adm... first in four years, and i... beer or 15 fags. No-one i... football at Craven Cot... want it, we must help ... directors stopped dip... there'd be no footba...

Come out of n... There are plenty c... at on our behalf, l... life in the system... part of that syst...

Yours sincerely

Eva Tenner,
London W1...

* No-one is ... up. Howev... only steep... likely to ... prices (a... is high... stay an... that is ... comp... brea... vid...

DAVE BASSETT, the creator of Wimbledon, has been known to stand up at a public dinner and pretend to exhibit himself.

Flashing, I think they call it.

PLAYERS

Wally Downes

is back in training

Flashing Blade

ALLAN MCKNIGHT'S QUIZ PAGE

Absolute first class SHITE!

YOU TOO CAN WIN A SUPER prize if you enter the NMTB special Relegation Competition. All you have to do is try your hand at the simple questions below.

(1) What is the goalkeeper doing exactly, and why?

(2) Where would you have rather been on this particular Sunday afternoon?

(3) "I didn't want to go to Wembley anyway because:
  a) probably wouldn't get a ticket anyway
  b) the buses are really bad on a Sunday
  c) it's only a Micky Mouse cup
  d) we can concentrate on relegation instead

The first correct entry out of the NMTB postbag will win a copy of Allan McKnight's new autobiography "I Came, I Saw, And The Ball Ended Up In The Back Of The Net."

Never Mind The Boleyn

HARROW BOROUGH
(All White)

8. Jimmy BOLTON
9. Richard EVANS
10. Francis CASSIDY
11. Wayne WANKLYN
12. Stuart HOWARD
14. Robert HAYNES

Peter Farr sent in this and comments; "...some players are on a hiding to nothing before they leave the dressing rooms!"

The West Ender

FOLLOW, FOLLOW

No8 50p

A RANGERS FANZINE

FORGIVE ME FATHER FOR I HAVE SIGNED...

MO SHOCK!

I've had enough of this warming-up. Why doesn't El Tel just stick us on now - Gazza looks knackered.

Arsenal Echo Echo

Hooligans Abroad

What I would like to know is if, as they say, all the country's hooligans were on the rampage in Germany last June; who was singing " Get Your Tits Out For The Lads" to.Whitney Huston during the Mandella concert. ????

Dear TLR

After two more International performances for Arsenal against Millwall recently, it is only fair to acknowledge the ability of this special player:

Mr TONY ADAMS portrait of a star. Tony was a special baby right from the kick off. His first distinctive action was a raised arm after two months. At five months came those first words 'D...d...d...Offside!

Tony aged 3.

Tony at the seaside.

And from Tony a great new game to play

The plot You are a central defender in Division 1. Running towards you is a dangerous centre forward.

The aim You must judge his run and time your counter run to the moment before the ball is released. Whether succesful or not you raise your right arm skywards, screaming 'Offside'

The prize Two ton of carrots and a place in Bobby Robson's World Cup squad.

Special tactics If the Ref isn't convinced, you look to the left, then to the right, and remembering the hours of teaching from George and Theo, you run forwards shouting 'Offside' thrusting your chest into the Refs face, pointing at a member of the opposition. If all else fails leve George to criticize the Ref after the game.

A.P. & C.A.

coming soon····

Warlock
in
BRING ME
THE HEAD OF
Vinnie JoneS
CERT.XXX

HE'D HAD IT TOO EASY TOO LONG: IT WAS TIME TO SEE WHO'S BOSS

"Excuse me for interrupting Mr Linesman, but I believe that that last attempt on goal there may have been a trifle offside"

The Spur

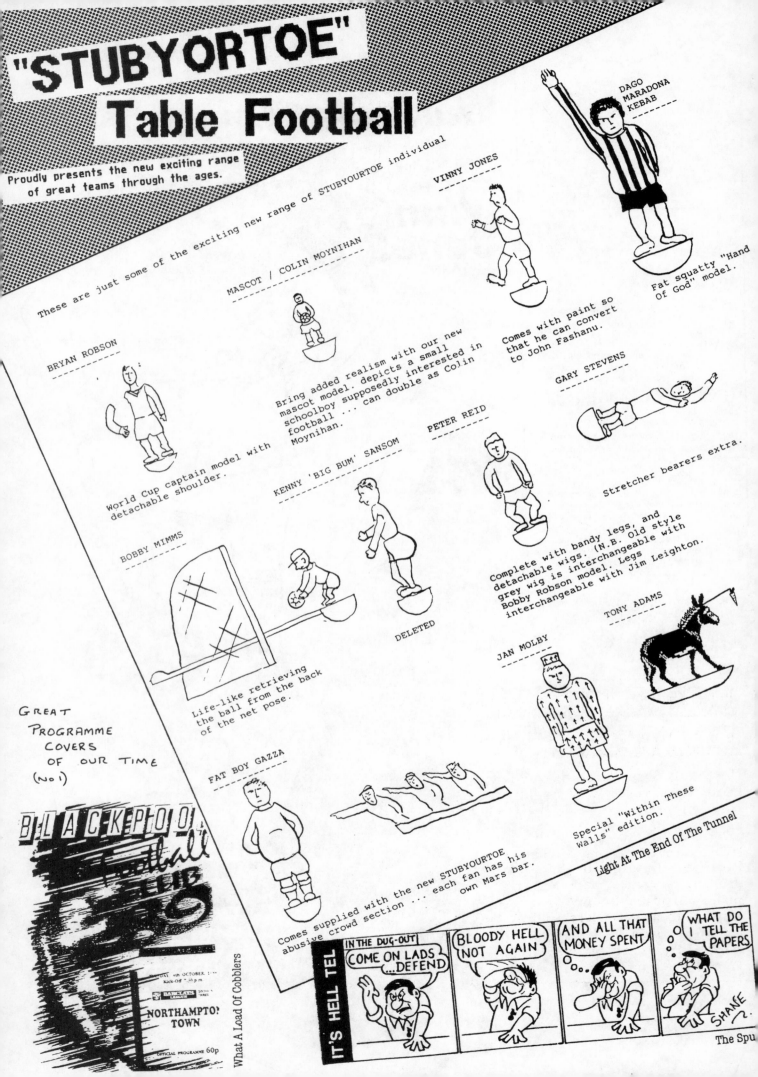

"STUBYORTOE" Table Football

Proudly presents the new exciting range of great teams through the ages.

These are just some of the exciting new range of STUBYOURTOE individual

DAGO MARADONA KEBAB
Fat squatty "Hand Of God" model.

VINNY JONES
Comes with paint so that he can convert to John Fashanu.

BRYAN ROBSON
World Cup captain model with detachable shoulder.

MASCOT / COLIN MOYNIHAN
Bring added realism with our new mascot model. depicts a small schoolboy supposedly interested in football ... can double as Colin Moynihan.

GARY STEVENS
Stretcher bearers extra.

PETER REID
Complete with bandy legs, and detachable wigs. (N.B. Old style grey wig is interchangeable with Bobby Robson model. Legs interchangeable with Jim Leighton.

KENNY 'BIG BUM' SANSOM
DELETED

BOBBY MIMMS
Life-like retrieving the ball from the back of the net pose.

TONY ADAMS

JAN MOLBY
Special "Within These Walls" edition.

GREAT PROGRAMME COVERS OF OUR TIME (No 1)

FAT BOY GAZZA
Comes supplied with the new STUBYOURTOE each fan has his own Mars bar.

Light At The End Of The Tunnel

BLACKPOO Football CLUB

NORTHAMPTON TOWN

SATURDAY 4th OCTOBER 1...
Kick-Off 3.00 p.m.

OFFICIAL PROGRAMME 60p

What A Load Of Cobblers

IT'S HELL TEL

IN THE DUG-OUT COME ON LADS ...DEFEND

BLOODY HELL NOT AGAIN

AND ALL THAT MONEY SPENT

WHAT DO I TELL THE PAPERS

SHANE

The Spu

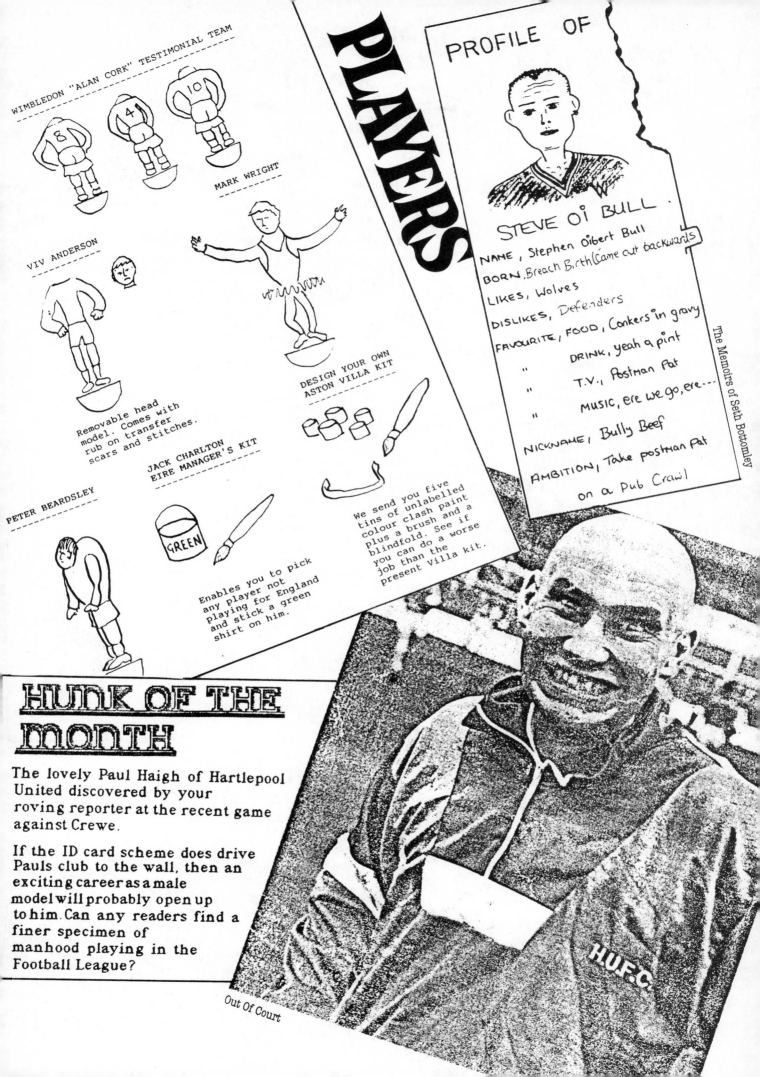

WIMBLEDON "ALAN CORK" TESTIMONIAL TEAM

MARK WRIGHT

VIV ANDERSON

DESIGN YOUR OWN
ASTON VILLA KIT

Removable head
model. Comes with
rub on transfer
scars and stitches.

JACK CHARLTON
EIRE MANAGER'S KIT

PETER BEARDSLEY

GREEN

We send you five
tins of unlabelled
colour clash paint
plus a brush and a
blindfold. See if
you can do a worse
job than the
present Villa kit.

Enables you to pick
any player not
playing for England
and stick a green
shirt on him.

PLAYERS

PROFILE OF

STEVE Oi BULL.

NAME, Stephen Oibert Bull

BORN, Breach Birth (Came out backwards

LIKES, Wolves

DISLIKES, Defenders

FAVOURITE, FOOD, Conkers in gravy

"   DRINK, yeah a pint

"   T.V., Postman Pat

"   MUSIC, ere we go, ere...

NICKNAME, Bully Beef

AMBITION, Take postman Pat
on a Pub Crawl

The Memoirs of Seth Bottomley

HUNK OF THE
MONTH

The lovely Paul Haigh of Hartlepool
United discovered by your
roving reporter at the recent game
against Crewe.

If the ID card scheme does drive
Pauls club to the wall, then an
exciting career as a male
model will probably open up
to him. Can any readers find a
finer specimen of
manhood playing in the
Football League?

H.U.F.C.

Out Of Court

PLAYERS

ACTION SHOT

Above:

EVER ALERT BEES 'KEEPER' PAUL PRIDDY BECOMES ANOTHER VICTIM OF THE GRIFFIN PARK PICK-POCKET.

Voice of the Beehive

---

the adventures of ' the

NOT SO FAMOUS FIVE

Julian, Dick and Anne, George and Timmy the dog

When people think of Hibs, five names spring to mind. Yes, for many, the names Smith, Johnstone, Reilly, Turnbull and Ormond are synonymous with Hibernian Football Club. Tales of their exploits become part of Easter Road folklore, and those of us who never saw them play were trained to pay homage to the memory of The Famous Five. However, in the not too distant past the arrival of another "Five" was heralded at Easter Road .....

Cast your minds back to the heady days of season 1985/86 - Hibs reached the Skol Cup Final and semi-finals of the Scottish Cup, and much was expected of the club the following season. Unfortunately, the precocious talents of Gordon Durie were exported to Chelsea, and Kenny Waugh pocketed a tidy sum as a result of the transfer. To be fair, signings were promised, and upon the eve of the new season, there were five new faces at Easter Road. It was heralded as the start of a new era, a stepping stone to success ... sales of season tickets rose dramatically ... and we stuffed the Huns on the opening day of the season! Sadly this was to be the only highlight of a depressingly drab season, and the new "Five" failed miserably to emulate the facts of their illustrious predecessors. But who were these men, and what has become of them?

BILLY KIRKWOOD - a tireless campaigner (i.e. he was pretty useless), who was elevated with remarkable rapidity to team captain. Unfortunately Billy never really settled and moved to Dunfermline.

STUART BEEDIE - joined Hibs from Passback United in the same deal that took Kirkwood to Easter Road. Unfortunately Stuart never really settled and moved to Dunfermline.

WILLIE IRVINE (the second) - bought to emulate the scoring prowess of his namesake. Unfortunately Willie never really settled and moved to ... well you guessed it.

MARK CAUGHEY - vast effort (apparently) was made by Kenny Waugh to sign this Irish World Cup "star". Unfortunately Mark never really settled and moved to Motherwell.

GEORGE McCLUSKEY - "Beastie" was a real bargain (i.e. he didn't cost a penny), and with years of experience behind him he looked .... well, he wooked pretty old and overweight to be honest. Unfortunately George really settled and remained with Hibs.

North-east Hiberni

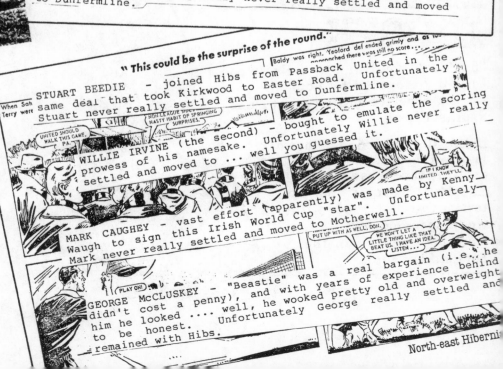

"I don't care if it is two in the morning, I want another 8 laps. Besides Ilkley Moor isn't that big!"

Following the unmitigated success of the Bobby Moore Story, (at least no libel writs to date on ED's doorstep), Booby's Page, employing Death on The Rock investigative journalism techniques, brings you an insight into the careers of two more soccer legends. Sit back for installment one of ....The Charlton Brothers.

BROTHERS IN BOOTS

Part 1: Anything But The Pit

Until recently the most famous brothers in soccer history, the Charlton boys began life in the Northumberland village of Hovis. "Times were hard then" says Jackie. "Our house were so cold our Mam would send us out to throw stones at local miners down at pit. We used to collect all coal they threw back at us for fire".

The boys were off to a flier as their mum (who bears an uncanny resemblance to Bobby Moore in Issue 4) was from the famous Milburn family. Cousin to Wor Jackie she remembers vividly the day her boys were born; Bobby with his hair swept to one side and Jackie with a shamrock in his mouth.

With the pit beckoning the boys dedicated their spare time to kicking a tennis ball around. Football, it had to be football; anything but the pit... but worse was to come ..Leeds

Next Issue:

Bobby lands a sponsorship deal with Brylcream.....
Jackie sees no future in it!

The Ugly Inside

In Defence Of Wimbledon

As I write, the football world is apparently heaving a huge sigh and hoping for that exquisite pearl among football's jewels, an all-Merseyside Cup Final. For yea, the pagans of Wimbledon have been vanquished and the true believers in the Superleague will inherit their birthright. Well, in between the cries of righteousness and the calls for Vinny Jones' execution, might I be permitted a brief stage whisper to suggest that, er, actually I quite like Wimbledon?

I suppose I finally got brassed off when the pundits told us, last year, that Liverpool had to win the Cup Final, "for the future of English football", and similar nonsense. I found watching Liverpool last year as exhilarating as anything I've seen in football. But if they could afford to spend £2.7 million on the front three, then doubtless Hartlepool would play like that! Certainly I would concede that Liverpool had a real commitment to playing classy football, and Wimbledon didn't, and neither position was totally imposed by the club's financial status. But the fact remains: as the richer clubs get richer, then they will buy the skilful players, and all the rest will have to find other means to pursue their goals. So the pundits who backed élitism in football have only themselves to blame.

The great majority of us who don't follow the Big Five are aware that there is far more to admire in footballers than skill. Who do you prefer, Gary Briggs or Jon Purdie? Even where skill is most admired, fans understand that. Ask a West Ham fan what they think of Billy Bonds! I always laughed when people whinged about Brazil going out of the World Cup. If you don't defend, i don't care if you can catch the ball in your teeth. Give me Enzo Bearzot's counter-attacking teams any day.

I prefer football based on passing to feet, to the long ball. That way a movement that breaks down can still be exciting and admirable rather than dull and frustrating. But each has its merits. I thought Wimbledon were marvellous when they won 5-2 here last year. The ball flew round the pitch like a pinball at times.

Are they a "dirty" team? Often. Is Jones an idiot? Yes. But are the great heroes of English football any better? I don't find Jones any worse than Reid, or McMahon, or Whiteside. All of those possess skills that attract the attention (and sycophancy) of the press. Does that make their sins less vile? The objection to Arsenal and Leeds, fifteen years ago, was that despite having wonderful players, they still chose to kick. Heighway didn't justify Smith then, and still doesn't.

The mouthiest teams in the League are Arsenal and Man.United, not Wimbledon. And the dirtiest is Everton. Of late, Jim Beglin, Ricky Hill and Kevin Summerfield have all been crippled for months by unpunished Everton tackles. Has this happened at Plough Lane?

I don't like to see teams kick. (I didn't like it when Oxford had seven men sent off in a season.) But I do like to see a team show the character to overcome their shortcomings in money and skill. I do like to see a team that brings on young players, and encourages black players. (Why is Fashanu considered a dirty player and Mick Harford isn't, eh?). And I do like to see a team that enjoys itself. Wimbledon's low attendances suggest that they don't play it the way people like to see it. But as long as they keep on taking the piss out of the Megateams, I'll keep on enjoying it.

Raging Bull

Cover Story

The SPUR
a heavenly

BACKWARD WITH ARSENAL

FIFTY NEW PENCE

NUMBER FIVE

An nah yer gerner bleeve us - an nah yer gerner bleeve us - an nah yer gerner bleevuuuuuus - we're gerner win the League

CHAMPIONS ELECT!

I still think we can win the League

Well, if Arsenal lose eight...

Where would we be this season without Chris Waddle. What a total genius this man is. Mere words would fail to do justice to his performance against Villa. I worship the ground he walks on and wish to impregnate myself with his offspring.

LOOKALIKES?

MARK

BIFFA

Has anyone noticed the uncanny resemblance between Mark Falco and Viz's Biffa Bacon?

In The Loft

The SOUP
Kidderminster Harriers fanzine

Special Welsh Cup edition

ISSUE TWO

It's the biggest crowd we've had all season...

What's in The Soup today?

THE MAG

ISSUE 7   ISSUE

50p

NEWCASTLE UNITED INDEPENDENT SUPPORTER'S MAGAZINE

WHAT A SHOWER!!

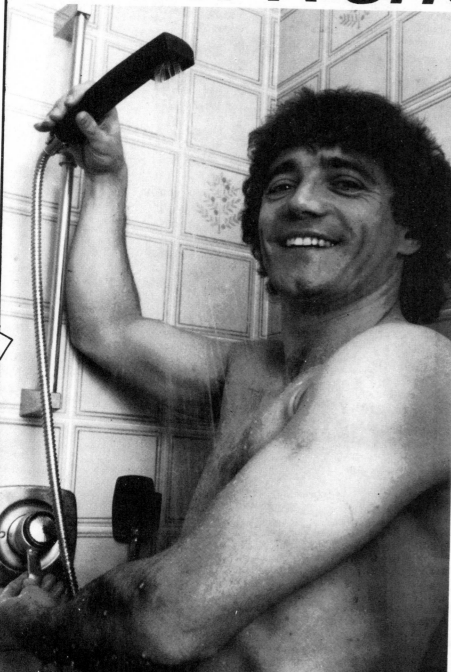

"This club should be buying players like Gascoigne and Beardsley, not selling them. If you sell class players like that you cannot keep producing them from out the bushes. Great area that it is for looking for talent and that maybe you have a great scouting system. Great players don't come along very often. Been very privileged here, they've had four or five in the last five years but they've sold them all.

You've got a nice stand but this won't look very good in the third division, will it? stands don't win football matches, they don't score goals and they don't pull people in. It just means when you've got a team good enough to pull them in it's nice to put them in something like this, but you cannot neglect your team.

I don't want them to go into the second division. I know how hard we worked to get them into the first and if the lads think it's hard to stay in the first division then they're going to be in for a shock next year if they go down to see how hard it is to get out of the second.

It's tough!"

Kevin Keegan, April 1989

BY SUPPORTERS FOR SUPPORTERS

Stick it on me centre parting, son

HERE COMES THE MANE AGAIN!
A "Horrendous Hotspur Haircuts" Special

No 1: The Chressy Wordel (The Christopher Roland Waddle)

(OK, I know you won't believe us, but before you go and tell all your mates that *The Spur* lacks originality (which it does anyway - Readers voice), may we just say that the title for this series was drawn up months before the *On The Ball* duo amazingly did something out of mainstream recently. Thank you.)

"Here comes the mane again, falling down his neck like a memory, falling down his neck like an old emotion. Is it paining you too?"

(Complaints about the atrocious introduction to this article should be addressed to the 'Disbelievingly Dreadful Department'. Cheers - Ed.)

The day? Saturday. The date? The eighth of December. The year? Nineteen eighty four ..... and Big Irving was watching you! Yes, it was three days on from our twice annual 'Are - you - blind - or - wot - Ref.; the - ball - was - well - over - the - line / that - was - a - penalty / miles - offside' removal from either of the two national Knockusout cups (this time The Milk of Human Kindness Cup at the grubby hands of Chris Turner's Sulund) and our heroes, The Spurs, were at home to our vanquishers best pals - the sleeping (more like in a coma) giants - Newcassel Yooneeted.

With Spurs playing in the ever so smart white/navy/white outfit for the last season before the "powers-that-be" broke one of The Tottenham Commandments, for some unknown reason, to make our boys resemble the inferior Leeds United - The Lilywhites were once again bearing under the strain as a certain 'Christopher Waddle' and his Jawdie "tim-mits" (team mates) playing in a cheerful all-grey strip (which pretty much resembled the mood of the day), were laying rip into our formation and into poor old Maxie 'Misunderstood' Miller, in particular.

Yesirree, this was 1984 and the height of fashion at the time was a haircut quite commonly known and popularly adopted on the terraces by many (excuse me whilst I vomit) 'casuals' as the infamous rowdy Brit on the cheap stuff abroad: "Perm the back, leave the front, shave the sides."

As we (Martin) shivered ourselves to death on The Shelf, dreaming of what might cheer us up at Highbury on January the first - that mysterious figure resembling an asthmatic Hunchback of Notre Dame, suddenly sprung up out of this agonising position - and with manic mane bouncing up and off his shoulder blades, tapped the ball delicately with his toes a few times, feinted one way then t'other, afore rounding with ease Mad Max in one fluid balletic more to arc the pigs bladder good low and hard into the far corner "beyond the despairing dive of Ray Clemence." When they say 'poetry in motion' (an often over-used phrase I find) goals only such as these are what should be meant. Sheer ecstasy! Or, er, joy rather as the Beeb would now have us say. There could not have been (particularly after our eventual 3-1 win!) a

The Spur

Horrendous Hotspur Haircuts No. 3: The Walshie Babes* (The Paul Walsh)
*aka The Janet

HOLSTEN

"Rapunzel, Rapunzel, let down thy long blonde hair"

Horrendous Hotspur Haircuts No. 2: The Mitch
(The Mitchell Anthony Thomas)
Mitchell in his Worzel days

single supporter within The Lane that day who would've failed to have been impressed by and liked that goal. In fact Peter Shreeve liked it so much - he bought the player!

Leaving, "St.Jims' Puk" in July in time for the new season 'That Geordie Basstud' all of a sudden became an acceptable and likeable human-being with a name of Chris Waddle until, that is, he failed to find his feet and form regularly, and we, the fans (yes we - and I'm talking to most here) all of sudden remembered that once more he had come from Newcastle (and in the true spirit of our generosity) "did - not - have - a - father - so - to - speak"; if you know what I mean Harold! Widdley, you could say, was well and truly piddleyed off, and so for a year searched high and low the playing fields of England for that moment of inspiration that would install the necessary stability required within his system to go on to become (but only once God had left) - The King of White Hart Lane.

But what could be done? What could our disjointed Geordie do? It is common folklore amongst us Tottenham lot, that it was at The Manor Ground on the 22nd of November 1986 that disillusioned Waddle and 'tim-mits' found their long searched for ability, direction, formation and belief. *The Spur* argues different (well you would you pretentious gits - Readers voice). On a date unknown to us Spurs fans but, we believe between the second and seventh of that month (so correct us if we are wrong) our Winger Widdley went to his barber (an unknown heroine/hero who cannot be thanked enough for removing that unsightly eyesore from around Chris' shoulders) and lo and behold out onto the street and the field at Marrow Road stepped to the adulating affectionate cries of: "Skin-ead, skin-ead," The (at that precise moment became in my heart) Next in Line to The Throne at The Lane.

From that day onward, Chrissy teased, tormented and tantalised just about any defence you should so care to dangle in front of his fine frame. Title-chases, cup runs and Ing-er-land places followed ad nauseam as our lads lapped up and revelled in the adulation we flung at them, and all this due to some marvellous piece of scissor work by some poor harassed hair-dresser on fire somewhere who has never been given that MBE she/he so richly deserved. Maybe next year! Only one other publication had noticed this as well and on Cup Semi-Final day at Villa Park its writer best summed up their observations in a study on the player, by stating that: "If you want to get ahead, get a haircut." His hair's heyday arrived on May the 16th 1987 for the (pass the hankies, please) FA Cup Final when his hair was so superbly shorn, one oth-erwriter went so far as to scribble that Wibbley looked like one of those fabulous jinky wingers from the Flickering Films of Fifties F.A. Fi-nals. Idolatry in its extreme!

But disaster struck! The team on commenc-ing what now seems a successful season in comparison to the present one we are gritting our teeth at, started to slip down the slipper slope from where it seems they haven't stopped sliding since. And the reason this? The ra decisions of Richard? The greed of Glen The depleating of D. Pleat? Nope. Chri forgot the trim which for nearly one whole y tenaciously held together the talents of Tot ham Hotspur.

I had my hopes when I went to Wembl August, but when he strode out from the tunnel my heart sunk further than I deemed possible. Not only was Wads hair longer but (Quick diall 999-Eds.) back in force was the hideous "long rat-tail like back, shave the front and sides". And it gets longer, and longer, and longer, and longer, and longer. And the longer it gets, the deeper our "crisis" grows.

Apart from bottom of the first division, where does this leave us? Well as much as we worship Weebles, sometimes we wonder when the re-alisation of this will click. For goodness (and your street cred's) sake Wobbles - get the scissors out for the lads, if only for the tortured soul of Terence.

And failing that? I bought this superb pair of garden sheers the other day. I hope to go to Wibbley's new book signing on Thursday as well.

Next: The Mitch (Marigold's stylist permit-ting).

BEFORE CLOUGH COULD CROSS THE BALL, DEVONSHIRE LASHED KIM WITH HIS UNFASHIONABLE SEVENTIES HAIRCUT...

Fortune's Always Hiding

PETER REID

DOCTORS' WARNING

The British Medical Association has issued a warning that the constant use of hair darkening agents can lead to premature falling out of the hair.

The main manufacturers have denied liability but are rumoured to have branched out into wigs.

The gentleman on the left said the matter was not in the hands of his solicitor, but was lying on the Goodison Park pitch.

Just Another Wednesday

1) THE DOUBLE SQUAD

Bob Wilson, as the keeper, the last line of defence, had a special responsibility to look good. A responsibility he took as seriously then as he now takes the responsibility to convince television viewers that the FA Cup is a far more exciting competition than the League. *(If the BBC were to end up with the sole exclusive rights to the Simod Cup, Bob, you can be sure, wouldn't flinch from his duty to promote it).* His tendency to roll up the sleeves of his goalkeeping sweater, which many stylists - if not hairstylists - considered a touch naff, was more than adequately balanced by the boldness and imagination of his hairstyle.

BOB: boldness and imagination

Bob chose the cheery Michael Caine look, minus, for practical rather than aesthetic reasons *(as befits the man)*, the Caine spectacles. Whilst purists might rue Bob's decision not to wear black-rimmed glasses during the Double season, most Arsenal supporters would reflect that Bob might have had a lot more difficulty during some of the rain-swept games of the winter, what with having to wipe his glasses clean all the time; would we have beaten Manchester City in the 5th round of the "more exciting" FA Cup if Bob had been bespectacled? I doubt it.

Bob's Cainian hairstyle clearly intimidated opposing strikers. Who could forget *(Sam Leitch and Jimmy Hill never let us)* Bob's brave, diving save at the feet of George Best, who was through with only the keeper to beat, at Highbury during the 4-0 win in the Championship, ("exciting, but not as exciting as the FA Cup")? Bob's bravery, his sense of timing, were keenly "spotlighted" by the experts, but what of the effect Bob's hairstyle had on the onrushing and just-zipped-back-from-Majorca-for-the-day Best? It threw him; he "bottled" it as soon as he laid eyes on Bob's bowed head hurtling towards him: Those tightly-knitted curls, packed in furrows with a religious uniformity destabilised the already unstable Best. How many games did that unforgettable hairstyle win for Arsenal? Hundreds!

The hairstyle remains unforgettable, simply because the mighty mediatic Bob is still giving it (or a modulated version of it at any rate) a lot of exposure, and rightly so. The taut, triangular formation at the top of the head has its roots firmly entrenched in classical

Greek mythology; Sophocles was said to have worn his hair Bob's way and it is no mere coincidence that Bob was once a schoolteacher.

Many people felt that **Bertie Mee** snapped up **Geoff Barnett** because of his name ("barnet") and his unashamed admiration for Bob's hairstyle: Geoff, who began his Arsenal career with a cropped look, (and saved a penalty with it in a crucial 0-0 away to Sporting Lisbon in the Fairs Cup), gradually allowed himself to experiment... and how! Hairstylists the world over have been split as to whether Geoff was "growing it out" or simply growing it. However, instead of growing longer, Geoff's hair grew upwards and outwards. There was speculation amongst Football Combination watchers that he was trying to grow the ultimate "Afro"; to fill his goal with hair, to carry so much hair that he would be wedged into the goal on Saturday afternoons. Geoff's dedication drove him to start using special floral creams and herbal treatments on his scalp (years before Body Shop) in an attempt to stiffen his roots.

GEOFF: Stiff roots

His dedication to adding another important weapon to his goalkeeping armoury was exemplary: Strong, tough hair which could repell even a **Bobby Charlton** thunderbolt. Alas, due to a serious injury to **Bob Wilson** in the 1972 semifinal against Stoke in the exciting FA Cup (much more exciting than the League!), Geoff was called into the first team ahead of his hairstyle schedule; sadly, he clearly wasn't ready. In another year, **Allan Clarke's** header would have simply thudded against Geoff's hair. But that's hairstyles, that's football, that's life. Nonetheless, Geoff wore perhaps the most special permanent wave of the 1972 FA Cup final, and to part of that excitement is not something easily taken away.

Blame it on his relative immaturity, but **Pat Rice**, it has to be said, is one of these people who give hairstylists the shakes. If everyone were like **Pat Rice**, so the saying went in the early Seventies, then there would have been no "hairdressing salons". It would have been barber shops and "do-it-yourself" haircut

kits. Pat favoured the Pudding Bowl look. Simple, short and unfussy. Whilst expected with a name like Rice, it is remarkable and a shade disappointing that he has steadfastly retained this same essential style throughout his career. Who knows, maybe the "change of life" will see a change of style?

RICE: Do-it-Yourself

Bob McNab, let's face it, had problem hair. He struggled to find a suitable barber during his Highbury career and never satisfactorily resolved the problem of what to do with the flyaway bits during windy conditions. Bob's problems were particularly acute at the start of a game before his forehead sweat started to mat his hair. Who could forget Bob's eversosexy sweeping movement with his left hand as he reorganised his folicles during a match? **Alf Ramsey** was impressed enough to select Bob as part of the World Cup squad for the Mexico 1970 World Cup, but when his hair dried out in the South American sun during the pre-World Cup tour, Bob's usefulness to the squad diminished and he was sent home. This new, blonder, more controlled hairstyle was immediately spotted by Independent Television and Bob became a member of what was (perhaps) the best "Panel" of all time: But that's another story.

BOB: Panel Beater

A bit of a coup for us really. Leading international coiffeur, *David Keith*, begins his look at great teams and the vital role that the players' hairstyles played in achieving success. Today he looks at the Double Squad and the variety of styles which helped the side achieve something which NO OTHER TEAM was capable of during the Seventies. Winning the League and FA Cup "Double". At last, the truth is out. Now read on...

Peter Storey and **Frank McLintock** were two players in the side who had absolutely no qualms about sporting "sideburns" or "sideboards" as they

FRANK: Complete sideboards

were referred to back then. Frank, as team captain, had the neater pair and chose to highlight them by leaving his ears exposed to the elements. But Frank was brave like that."

Snout" on the other hand, in stark contrast with his ferocious on-the-field image, was often seen with a large bunch of hair over either ear, negating the full effect of the sideboard whilst giving the impression that he was wearing a pair of old fashioned headphones. Possibly this was to afford him scope when challenged by referees, *("Sorry ref, didn't hear the whistle - I was listening to my new David Bowie LP")*, whilst there again it might have been solely to tempt opponents into calling him a "cissy" or a "pansy". Whatever the reason, without Storey sideboards keeping his wits about him, the "Double" would never have been won.

STOREY: "Call me a cissy if you dare"

Peter Simpson: The only player in the team (discounting **Jon Sammels**) who confidently sported a fringe - Simpson was never a fringe player. However, his failure to make the England side might

HIGHLIGHTS

be explained by his choice of haircut. Ramsey - an outright "baldie" - had a distinct preference for bald or balding players: **Cohen, Wilson, Stiles** and the **Charlton boys** as well as the high-foreheaded **Bobby Moore**.

SIMPSON: Fringe benefits

George Armstrong: Perhaps his unusually large head and pugilist features helped give the impression that he was totally without a hairstyle. Armstrong's hair just seemed to grow and flow, into his eyes, ears, mouth, you name it, "Geordie's" hair was everywhere. A separate groundsman had to be employed at Highbury during the Double season, just to collect the flyaway bits. Armstrong was Arsenal's heavy metal merchant - more so than Charlie.

ARMSTRONG: Pugilistic features

Charlie George: Oh dear, oh dear... Charlie! Lank, flyaway hair before the days of popular styling mousse and gel. What shouldn't you do? Grow it long and/or have a perm. Keep it short is the message and Charlie started well enough, with a nice, neat short back and sides. Then **Susan Farge** came along and encouraged him to grow it. Did he say he wouldn't cut it until Arsenal had won the Double? No. He just let it grow. Outrageous. However, you did get used to it. Charlie's problems started when he moved to Derby. Oh dear... the worst perm in living memory; it became so difficult to believe in him, at least, as he was a Derby player, we didn't really have to it... but admit it, didn't you secretely

hope that he'd come back? (With his hair straightened out, of course).

CHARLIE: Pre-perm, pre-gel

George Graham, John Radford and **Ray Kennedy:** Finally, the "Double Strike Force": Immediatley striking about these three deadly goalscorers is that they all wore their hair high on the forehead. A popular theorey was that this was in defer-nce to the bald management team of **Bertie Mee** and **Don Howe**, but there was a far more practical reason than this.

GRAHAM: High forehead

Having seen the success of **Alan Gilzean** and his "headed flicks" up the road at Tottenham, coach and budding stylist Don Howe suggested at the start of the season that the three big men, the "receivers" of Armstrong's crosses, should keep the hair off the forehead in order to ensure that their headers (and there were many of them) were accurate. It worked; all three scored with prolific regularity: Significantly, it was Kennedy's bullet header

KENNEDY: Bullet header

which clinched the Championship at White Hart Lane, prompting **Alan Gilzean** to remark, "Hair of the Dog". Note how **Don Howe** at **Wimbledon** insists that his players wear their hair short!

RADFORD: Sweaty

But one shouldn't forget the others; the neatly turned out Jon Sammels' hairstyle was very in keeping with his character; neat and tidy. (Jon was voted the League's "best-looking player" at least once in my memory, beating George Best, probably on the strength of his hairstyle).

There was John Roberts, another neat and tidy cut. But pride of place must go to Eddie Kelly, without question, the player in this squad who resolutely refused to be tied down or restricted by hairstyle culture. Eddie's frizzy locks resulted in him trying a variety of styles, short, medium to long, but always, absolutely always, with a powerful sideburn.

KELLY: Variety

An Imperfect Match

NEWCASTLE UTD.

NEWCASTLE UTD

NEXT T

TH

PERMA

WAY

Dad, what's a Cup Final

The Mag

Who's the bank clerk in the black?

THE REFEREE'S GUIDE TO ANFIELD

After our recent victory at Liverpool, I found on the terraces a photocopied sheet bearing the above heading. I was shocked and stunned when I read this document and felt it was 'The Mag's' duty to reproduce the text in full.

1) Liverpool play in red.

2) As you know, Anfield is the home of many fine traditions and one of these is that we are unbeatable at home. Any dubious decision in our favour is merely your way of upholding this fine and honourable tradition.

3) Try not to feel pressurised by the 40,000 souls who are screaming for your blood. Remember these are just those fun loving scousers you've read about in the papers. Rumours of powdered glass in your half-time bovril and phone calls to the wife about that bit of stuff you've got with you today are precisely that - rumours.

4) Liverpool cannot concede free kicks as the players are under strict instructions not to kick the opposition (or certainly not while you are looking). We must confess we did have one player who transgressed this law and he was soon sent packing to Italy. (It is rumoured he is now mutilating Catholics in Glasgow).

5) Today's opponents are basically honest men but are liable to give away needless penalties anywhere up to 5 yards outside the box. We urge you to be on your guard and not to hesitate to do your stuff. (Remember the tradition).

6) There is nothing more embarrassing for a TV commentator when he defends a neck high lunge by McMahon or Whelan as 'enthusiastic' then you come over and caution the player. Please remember you are on TV and you should do your utmost to assist the bullshit of Moore/Motson.

7) To assist you in identifying the latest Liverpool goalscorer please note that Rush is slightly uglier than Aldridge and also smells of garlic.

8) Please do not be alarmed that Barry Venison carries a lump of shit around with him, being a Sunderland fan he simply uses it for identification.

9) If you like to listen to the pre-match build up on the local radio then the set in your room is pre-tuned. Do not re-adjust if you get a high pitched interference as this usually just means that Emlyn is having chat with someone just outside your door.

10) If all is well, I'll see you in the boot room later.

John Scorfield

I believe Viv Anderson has never played dirty,

I believe Jan Molby was only doing thirty,

I believe Alan Harper is pretty,

I believe Kenny Dalglish is witty,

I believe Vinny Jones is polite and ireffectual,

I believe Steve McMahon's an intellectual,

I believe Bryan Robson has given up booze.

But I can't believe Terry Darracott's in charge of the Blues.

The Mag

YOU ARE THE REF

Follow, Follow

Try the following teasers and test your refereeing skills against our resident SFA expert, Blind Pew.

1) Alex McLeish machetes Ally McCoist to death on the touchline and buries him in a shallow grave.
Dou you:-   a) Send McLeish off
          b) Book him
          c) Send off McCoist for leaving the field for leaving the field of play without permission

2) The entire Aberdeen defence jump on Kevin Drinkell in the penalty box.
You decide:-
a) Penalty to Rangers
b) Indirect free kick in the box
c) Book Drinkell for provocation

3) After a decision goes against him Jim Bett aims a vocal barrage at you using a microphone and a 500 watts per channel PA system
Do you:-
a) Book him
b) turn on your deaf aid
c) Apologise profusely and reverse your decision

4) Charlie Nicolas has his tights laddered by Gary Stevens.
Do you:-
a) Ignore it and play on
b) Send Stevens off and provide him with an escort of Aberdonians shouting abuse in his ear
c) Award Aberdeen a free kick

5) Alex Smith shouts something from the touchline which you only vaguely hear, but the diatribe includes the words "kill", "maim" and "destroy."
Do you:-
a) Call him over and book him
b) Ask him for a written complaint, in joined-up writing
c) Stop the game while Aberdeen a chance to change into hob-nailed boots Points per answer:- a) 0 points
              b) 3 points
              c) 5 points

How did you do ?
0-3   You obviously know the rules of football and could never be a referee
4-24   You could be Louis Thow
25   Well done Willie Miller

Paper Roses

Above: The board presents a brief synopsis of their strategy for avoiding relegation this season.

Rats chased by Souness

By ROY FEE

The Independent

Not The View

GRAEME   EX-WIFE

Gordon Reid

LECHER

Every Boxing Day at 11 a,m I'm at South Bank to watch the local derby with Whitby Town.Its always freezing and full of mad woolie backs supporting Whitby and theres a strange smell in the air,Its a sort of mixture of B.S.C,fish,new after shave and new gloves.The footballs crap of course except for a couple of years ago when Eddie Gray and Peter Lorimer played for Town,Gray hit the bar from 30 yards and Lorimer scored from a free kick like he used to on Match of The Day. Theres nobody famous this year to spoil the terribleness of the game the best fighters normally win.Whitby went 2-0 up thanks to two howlers from the young gadgie making his home debut.What a Banker.Whitby were so surprised they lapsed into realms of incompetence only hinted at previously and snatched defeat from the realms of victory just in time to lose 3-2. Bobby Scaife scored the winner.He used to be on Boros books and also had spells at Hartlepuddle and Rochdale.He spoilt the game by being able to pass properly and shoot straight. AIl this excitement for a quid.The oxo is cheap and the pies are hot.And sometimes,but only sometimes,your car is still there when you leave the ground.
BEACHED WHALE

A jubiliant Dundee boss Dave "Coco" Smith introduces

Fly Me To The Moon

his new signing

to the Dens

GROUND SAFETY

When Sunday Comes

Pre-disaster

SEASONS REVIEW

Another disasterous campaign for Liverpool, following the failings of 1986/87, where The Reds could only finish runners-up in two competitions, this was another poor season. Although the league was won by a mile, the F.A.Cup Final was lost, hence confirming Wimbledon as the best team in the country. A season with many talking points, apart from the games themslves.

Severely crushed at Derby County, plenty of room at Wimbledon. Blackburn Rovers meat pies were really good, but Chelsea's burnt burgers aren't that tasty. It was great fun at Luton outsinging the home fans, and for some reason there was quite alot of room as well. The police at Nottingham inspired no confidence whatsoever, but then that's the worst of a pretty bad bunch. Not being allowed into Portsmouth with a ticket aggravated a few fans. Seeing the gates being run was pretty funny, as long as no-one was hurt, but there was no where near enough room allocated to Liverpool. The number of fans Liverpool took everywhere was impressive, the number of fans Luton took to Anfield was pathetic, not so Newcastle and Chelsea, who show Liverpool up without even trying. There was big disappointment at Watford who can usually be relied upon to supply some absolutely ludicrous pre-match or half time entertainment. The people of Newcastle were very helpful to us, the police weren't quite so helpful (eh Ben). Coventry still offers nothing. The "pitch" at Derby is pretty bad, but its best, Norwich just offers nothing. The "pitch" at Derby is pretty bad, but at the end of the season Anfield was still going strong. The organisation at Wembley is still unbelievable, is clueless too kind a word? Prices in London still appear, how do you say, a little high. After you've worked out Hampton Court Maze you can spend the afternoon at Southampton, Stoke is another away section, a side, as opposed to an end, which doen't give the best view, one of the best views I got was next to The Shelf at Spurs, standing at the base of what I think was the floodlight. The queue outside Arsenal brought questions about the organisation, as did the zig-zag path home, the one open gate at West Ham still worries me. As for the worst grounds, The Manor, Butlins , (Kenilworth Road), The Dell, The Baseball Ground, Carrow Road and not forgetting the spacious Goodison Park. The best, Villa Park, Maine Road, and really putting Anfield to shame Hillsborough.

hillsborough:very impressive, a shame they don't allow cameras

BRANDED as sub-human:
SHOVED ABOUT like cattle:
LEFT TO DIE in wire cages—

The Crooked Spireite

HOW MUCH LONGER WILL THEY TREAT US LIKE THIS?

Dear Oatcake,

　　　　After seeing the terrible scenes from Hillsborough two weeks ago, I feel that I must write to you concerning the South Yorkshire Police.

　　　　I was one of the many STOKIES who travelled up to Barnsley in the FA Cup replay. At kick off time there were still 1500-2000 STOKIES outside the ground. The Police kept asking the STOKE fans to move along but there was just no room, so at half-time they just opened the gates and let the remainder of our fans in.

　　　　The same tragedy could have happened at Oakwell that Tuesday night.

　　　　Yours Faithfully
　　　　Andy Seabridge
　　　　Leek Road
　　　　Cheadle
　　　　Stoke on Trent

PS Well done lads for donating £100 to the disaster fund.

　　　　　　　The Oatcake

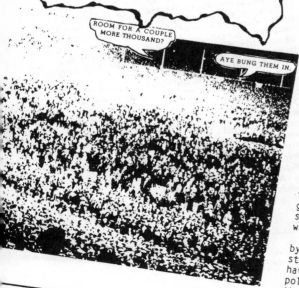

ROOM FOR A COUPLE MORE THOUSAND?

AYE BUNG THEM IN.

Not The View

As We View It

Crowded Out

As we flocked to Celtic Park for the game which would finally clinch the league last season we were all in good spirits and all set for a great day out.

Unfortunately, for many people that day, the desperate crushes outside and inside the ground, spoiled what would otherwise have been a perfect day.

Who do we have to blame for the scandalous lack of forethought, planning and stewarding that day?

Such were Celtic's crowds in the run-in to last season's championship as people from all over the country tried to join in the centenary league-winning celebrations, that it seems almost inconceivable that the club did not expect anything less than a sell-out on the day of the Dundee game.

That being the case, there is no excuse for not making the game itself all-ticket. Crowd control outside the stadium leaves enough to be desired without the prospect of hordes of fans faced with the prospect of a lock-out.

Having decided in their infinite wisdom not to make the game all-ticket, the onus then fell on whoever was responsible for this to ensure that supporters were able to make their way safely into the ground under proper supervision. Quite clearly this was not the case.

Stewards were conspicuous by their absence (even extra staff hired for the day might have helped), while the mounted police, never very popular at the best of times, helped

everybody by trampling on their toes and making sure the crushes swayed from side to side occasionally, just to relieve the boredom.

The net result of all this bungling incompetence on the part of the officials responsible was a situation full of danger and fear for those of us unlucky enough to be caught up in it.

Meanwhile the surveillance cameras were presumably capturing everything on video for the benefit of the police officers who sit in the comfort of the press box; or were they too busy trying to zoom in on somebody having a pee in the Jungle so that they could direct two of their colleagues to lift the villain?

Even after the game had started fans continued to pour in through the gates, while the directors benevolently looked on as the inevitable overflow onto the track happened. Do these guys actually ever know when the ground is full?

The sickest joke of all was when the official crowd figure was released. Well-used as we are to swallowing these figures, even the most gullible of board cronies must have let out a gasp of astonishment when the press informed us that the crowd was 60,800; spot on the capacity, the gatemen must be better at counting than we thought.

Still, the board say it was 60,800, and who are we to argue?

The bottom line is that once again the fans were treated with contempt. When this attitude is no longer prevalent among the people in charge of the club then there will be no more need for depressing editorials like this one.

Panic on the streets of London

The incidents outside the grounds of West Ham and Arsenal this season as people queued up to gain admission I could and probably should have made a major article in this issue. However, the two letters printed below are representative of the huge bundle we received, and say most of the things we would have said.

I'm sure I wont be the only Spur to say a few words about the debacle at our friendly neighbours, those chirpy Cockneys from West Ham. Before you choke on your beer, I'm not talking about the match itself. No, obviously that was great entertainment, or what we saw of it was anyway.

Firstly I've got to admit that we didn't get into our queue until around 2.30, due to most of our group wanting another beer (me included). We still felt we had loads a time, little did we know.

As usual at West Ham we had to negotiate the Heathrow style metal detectors. There was a great number of Spurs fans still outside desperate to get in. Unfortunately, this combination led to the detectors being knocked down and immediately becoming a dangerous obstacle to overcome. One of my mates who was right in the middle of this ludicrous situation, later told of how one of our beloved boys in blue told him to stand up straight which was a physical impossibility with the hundreds of rightly angry fans pushing this way and that behind him. He even said in the pub afterwards that he'd feared for his life.

If this weren't enough, a lunatic on a horse came into the fray (putting more fans at risk of injury), to get everyone against the wall to queue up yet again. This was done without any prior warning and could have turned very easily into an ugly situation. During this, one of our group was taken away, for the dubious offence of voicing his disgust at the old bill's dangerous and needless action.

By now the match was 20 minutes old. We now realised that there were only 2 or 3 turnstiles to accommodate the large number of, now furious, Spurs fans. When we eventually got in it was quite clear that our section was vastly overcrowded whilst there were still large numbers outside.

Surely when any London club with large support i.e. ourselves, Millwall, Chelsea, or even the arse go to Upton Park they should get all the South Bank. What makes it more annoying is that when the hammers come to our place, they get all of the Park Lane, no question.

I've travelled away for 5 years now, and I've never seen anything as potentially dangerous as this. Some sections of the police don't seem to give a monkey's about the safety of football fans. Something has got to be done to solve this problem before someone gets killed.

John Ford
Woodford Green
Essex

I'm absolutely dreading the arrival of the new I.D. card scheme after trying to gain entry to the West Ham ground on 17/12/88. At 2.40 pm we arrived at the visiting supporters' end to be greeted by those appalling metal detectors the Upton Park police seem to favour so highly each year. I mean, scores of Spurs supporters having to channel through three of these monstrosities is ludicrous. Then after getting through that little fiasco, the West Ham officials in their infinite wisdom decide to lock the turnstiles at about 2.55pm creating a bottleneck outside the ground. Supporters, not knowing this behind, start to push forward as kick-off time is drawing near. Finally, as the Spurs fans start kicking the doors, one points out, "Well, if you lock the f—ing doors at 3.00 you expect them to break the doors down." So the flood gates open and I get pushed straight passed the turnstiles into a brick wall. After spending some time with my nose flat against this wall, some helpful, kind, considerate Spurs supporter graciously grabs me by the scruff of the neck and hauls me into the general direction of the turnstile (cheers pall). Then to add insult to injury, I hand over my fiver (20 minutes into the game), only to be told, "Sorry darling, no change." God knows what it's going to be like when the stewards have to check each card. I think I'll arrive at noon. Thank God (or should I say, Mabbsy and Mitch), we won.

Lisa W.
Ickenham
Middlesex

Sheffield United have put one over Wednesday by being the first city club to install an executive box. After much searching the club managed to find a supporter who had attended three consecutive matches, and awarded him the Supporter Of The Year Trophy, the prize being to watch the opening match from the comfort of the new executive box.

Here we picture our happy Unitedite during the game. However, we are not sure whether he is reacting to events on the pitch or whether he has suddenly realised that, due to an architectural design fault, there is an automatic time lock on the door and he will be unable to emerge until next May.

Just Another Wednesday

LIFE BEHIND BARS . . . . .

If you are reading this at Griffin Park take a look around you, notice anything unusual? Well, if you watch all of your football at Brentford then you won't have noticed the gradual introduction of fencing at most league grounds over the past few years. Theses fences which are of course introduced whether or not the paying customers want them are intrusive to say the least. Anybody whose been to Bristol Rovers new 'ground' or Aldershot recently will know that they completely spoil the view, especially for the away supporters. Probably the worst example I've seen is at Northampton where the away supporters cage would not be out of place in the most primitive of zoos. It helps to ensure that away supporters can only see about 2/3 of the pitch (I hope their supporters appreciate what a real ground is like in January). What are they there for? How many times have pitch invasions taken place at Aldershot or Twerton Park? Can't the vast numbers of police who attend games now not keep a few looneys off the pitch?

So far at Brentford we have escaped having any fences at all. I really hope that this continues. Given that most of the standing accommodation is low down now, having a 7 foot high spiked fences would ruin the view of the majority of fans with the only consolation being protection against Keef Millen's shots! I hope that if we ever get promoted the club are not panicked into putting up the dreaded wire. They should follow the example of West Ham which doesn't seem to have done them much harm!

Nick Porter.

For what it's worth, the day started off badly as I was stopped from selling behind the South Bank as I was "causing an obstruction". This was in a large road, where I was selling on one pavement, and my Dad the other, and the road itself had been completely blocked off to traffic at both ends. We joined the infamous queue at 2.45 and after the storming of the metal detectors, but still no signs of entry by 3.15, we went round to the North Bank and shut our mouths for an hour and a half.

Seemingly West Ham couldn't be bothered to pay for other turnstile operators. Judging by Lisa's letter you would think there would be a queue of applicants as the perks are so high. Merely claim to have no change, and pocket the difference.

On the subject of the detectors, are metal objects in proliferation? Whilst one object is too many and could cause injury or even death, you could easily throw coins if you wanted to. The detectors were a waste of time, and a dangerous waste of time at that. Perhaps they were a trial run for the membership scheme and the results, as the great Enoch Powell once said, "fill me with a deep sense of foreboding."

The Spur

Out of Court presents.....ACTION FROM BRIGHTON v AFC BOURNEMOUTH !!!

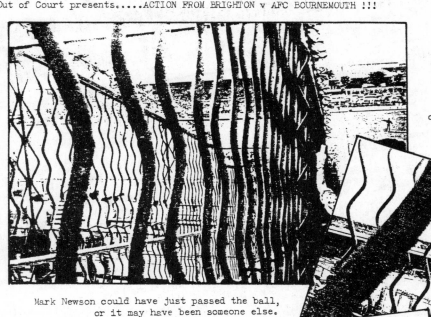

Mark Newson could have just passed the ball,
or it may have been someone else.

Out Of Court

Er, the game may have started and someone may
have just passed the ball to someone else,
maybe.

* * * * * * *

Us Bournemouth fans are lucky people, it only
cost us £4-00 to spend an afternoon looking at
modern sculpture, while the poor Brighton
fans spent fifty pence less and all they saw
was the game.

Mick C Sunny, Sunny,
Suffolk Reds.

GROUND SAFETY

SATURDAY APRIL 15TH

Coming the day after yesterday's tragedy at Hillsborough, this is the most
difficult piece I have had to write as Editor of "Size 10 1/2 Boots".

My intention at 3 0'Clock yesterday was to watch an afternoon's football -
Barrow v Gainsborough Trinity, HFS Loans League - and to report the details in
this magazine. However, when the news emerged of the disaster at Sheffield,
the game I had come to see seemed irrelevant. I had hoped to write about
Barrow's likely promotion to the GM Vauxhall Conference, but instead simply
want to offer the Supporters of Liverpool FC and the bereaved families our
most sincere sympathy.

For me, yesterday's events were made more shocking and possibly had an even
greater impact because of 2 personal visits to Hillsborough. On hearing the
news I immediately remembered my first visit to Hillsborough. It was at the
FA Cup Semi-Final between Tottenham and Wolves that the Kick-Off was delayed
to give more time for the Spurs supporters to gain entry into the ground at
the Leppings Lane end. I recalled Tottenham fans being crushed below on the
terraces as we sat in the comfort of the seats. The consequences in 1981,
fortunately, were not fatal, but a number of people were injured and
distressed. The delayed Kick-Off in '81 might have prevented there being
fatalities, but why was the start not delayed yesterday?

Many non-football goers will be quick to put the burden of blame on the
spectators. But surely these very people are the ones to blame, more than
anyone. Their ignorance has put pressure on the Government to introduce the
ludicrous and unacceptable 'Football Spectator Bill' to rid society of the
'hooligan problem' that the media has become so obsessed with, and largely
created itself. Whilst football supporters' interests of safety, comfort and
ground amenities have been ignored, the media (ie non-football goers) have
latched on to the greatly exaggerated problem of hooliganism, and advocated the
installation of fences and cages to control the "animals" who attend matches.

Whatever sensible actions are taken in the future to increase ground safety
(ie removal of perimeter fences and pens, to allow access to the pitch in
emergencies, and movement on the terraces), an ID card scheme would make such
measures a waste of time. The inevitable build-up of people on big match-days
as Kick-Off time approaches, even with adequate policing, would be likely to
produce further tragedies.

Today, replaying the Cup S/F is being debated. Many newspapers have suggested
that the FA Cup should be scrapped this year in respect of those that have
died, and those families grieving. Nothing could be more inappropriate, and
this is a typical over-reaction from the media. The Cup match, however
painful for players and supporters, should go ahead. 'Life must go on', and
football is very much part of the life of the City of Liverpool.

This issue of "Size 10 1/2 Boots" was actually completed a few hours before
yesterday's tragedy at Hillsborough, and this article has been written in
haste to include before printing because of its importance. I have decided,
after careful consideration, to not omit the 'Playing Away' feature, which
describes a very happy day spent at Anfield a month ago, or the light-hearted
piece concerning Nottingham Forrest.

The Editor

Size 10½ Boots

GROUND SAFETY

It wasn't easy, It wasn't easy, Getting in, ...At the Lane

21st October 1987

30 Dene Road
Guildford
Surrey
GU1 4DD

Dear Tottenham,

We would like to appeal in the strongest terms to the treatment of Arsenal fans at last Sunday's game at White Hart Lane. Year in, and year out we are forced to queue, and queue and queue still further to get into the ground. Year in, year out we bring thousands of supporters but year in, year out we are herded through three, maybe four turnstiles.

For Sunday's game I, along with three friends, turned up at 1.45, time enough I thought to be in position and settled before the game commenced. However fifty minutes later it's started and we have not even seen our turnstiles, let alone got near them.

In frustration I pull away from the queue and decide, having lost my mates in the melee, to try and get in with the Spurs fans. To my disgust I turn the corner and see four of five turnstiles with just a handful of people going in. Further down the road they are totally unused. £1 pay my money (no wonder you made such a big profit with admission prices like those) and entered the ground. A policemen asked me who I supported and I was shown the way to the empty piece of terracing in the corner just as we took the lead.

Later on in the evening when I was re-united with friends they told me they were escorted to the upper terracing in the corner at about 3.0. They had missed a third of the game and all three goals.

We have put up with this treatment for a long time, last season's Cup matches were especially bad, because we always win.

But when you miss a third of the match, all the goals and still have to pay an exorbitant £4.50 you tend to get a little agitated. We would like to know why this happens, continues to happen and what are you going to do about it.

Yours Sincerely

Arsenal

ARSENAL

Arsenal Echo Echo

BLACK SATURDAY

A day that began with such promise turned out to be one of the saddest in my years as a football supporter. Norwich's semi-final against Everton at Villa Park was the biggest match of the majority of the fans' lives (with respect to the Milk Cup), and the 19,000 City fans on the long road to the Midlands made a spectacular sight - green and yellow everywhere.

On arrival at Aston, we walked around the ground, where Everton and City fans mingled freely, and at 2 o'clockish , we entered the massive Holte End where the festivities really began. 10,000 inflatable Canaries were hoisted proudly as the teams came out, and at this moment we were blissfully unaware of the carnage that was going on 70 miles up the road at Sheffield.

Our match was played out with plenty of gusto, from players and fans alike, and it was, at the time, bitterly disappointing that Norwich lost a game that they didn't deserve to - they had played below their best , but still better than Everton, luck was just not on our side. Our knowledge of events at Hillsborough was that the game had been suspended due to , serious overcrowding' and later postponed, but even on leaving Villa Park we still didn't know that anyone had died there. The predictable fighting broke out outside the ground, and some unpleasant scenes erupted, but were soon quelled by an efficient police force. It wasn't until we got back to the car and set off east along the M6 that we heard the full extent of the disaster, although I knew that there had been some fatalities, after seeing the truly sickening sight of one car load of Norwich ,supporters , actually celebrating the fact. I'd like to think that even those dickheads felt sorry and sad later on when they realised the full extent of the disaster.

The toll at that time stood at 74, and it just seemed totally incompre-hensible that so many had died. Stunned disbelief was the feeling in our car load, and already the feeling of disappointment at losing our semi had changed into real sadness. We stopped off in Market Harborough to try and cheer ourselves up, and met some Leicester fans in the pub, who had earlier been slugging it out with the Chelsea fans at their match, and they were equally shocked about Liverpool's tragedy. All thoughts of further scrapping had gone, and they greeted us with a friendly chorus of " You're gonna win ++++ all as usual ". We had to agree with them, but it really didn't matter. A few bevvies and a biriyani improved the spirits, but the over-riding memory of the day was one of great sadness.

The Citizen

Marital writs...

My wife says all I care about in life is the Harriers. Now she has left me, saying she wants a divorce. I asked her what were the grounds for this rash decision. She said: "Barnet, Sutton, Wycombe, Runcorn and Fisher Athletic for starters." I wonder if any of your other readers have an amusing story about how the Harriers ruined their marriage?

D. Vorce,
Bewdley.

The Soup

When Saturday Comes

The Half Decent FOOTBALL Magazine

June 1989 No. 28

50p

Hillsborough: Unanimous Verdict

Dear Sir

These Liverpool Derby games are a complete con. Derby never play in them! No wonder Liverpool are top of the League!

R Maxwell

The Lion Roars

Dear "H,H & H",

I recently purchased issue 2 of the mag and noticed a great improvement, although there are still a few 'weak spots'. The biggest, I think, is the continuing nostalgia/adherence to the idea that we are part of Yorkshire. I (and many other people) consider Hull to be part of Humberside, thank you, and are well pleased about it. I'm sure none of us were truly happy living in the same County as Leeds or Sheffield (not to mention Rotherham and Halifax).

There are a thousand reasons to be glad to be out of all that White Rose crap. I for one do not wear a cloth cap, belong to a brass band, own a whippet, eat black pudding, talk with a wally accent, indulge in sexual activity with a sheep or any of the other activities undertaken by a typical Barnsley or Huddersfield-type Yorkshireman.

It should be clear that those of us east of Goole have nothing in common with the 'millfolk', 'miners', 'clog-wearers', Hovis-ad brigade apart from the fact that we once shared a name. Now we have Humberside - a much more apt description of the place we live. No slag-heaps, cobble-stoned pit villages or steelworks, no mill towns, just good honest Humberside scenery of flat field, our river & our beautiful bridge.

I can only think that people still wishing to be part of Yorkshire have seen too many episodes of Emmerdale Farm or drunk too much Tetleys. They should wake up and count their blessings.

Humberside is to Yorkshire what Merseyside is to Lancashire - a place with better football & better people than it's bigger woolyback neighbours.

HULL CITY - PRIDE OF HUMBERSIDE !

'Boothferry Ultra'

Hull, Hell and Happiness

(1986)

WE WANT TO HEAR FRO

Write to:
The Mag
Unit 11
25 Low Friar Street
Newcastle
NE1 5UE

Well Done Brian

I have just watched an idiot run on the pitch at Forest and start punching some of his own supporters, now even the Leeds fans don't do that. Just when everything had quietened down, the "Edwina Currie" of football wipes out all the good work done by the supporters and the F.S.A. etc. We have even had some good publicity for a change e.g. inflatables, fancy dress etc: by the Manchester City supporters. Now the press have had a field day. Thatcher and the miniature must have thought it was their birthday, "look shortarse, even the managers are at it now, we'd better give them I.D. cards as well". We were even getting some of the Tories on our side and there was talk of a rebellion in the Lords. What chance have we now and all because the "Almighty Brian" decides to become a football vigilante. What I find amazing is that there will be no action taken by the police, this man must be above the law. The following day Clough bragged about what he had done in the Wapping Whopper and how he would do it again. If it had been anybody but Brian Clough, they would have had the book thrown at them. It's a good job it wasn't John Fashanu or Vinny Jones. Get your 9 quid ready for your membership card.

Wayne Norris

A Match Day In The Life Of Vincent Jones

6-7 am Breakfast: six-inch nails, broken glass, two pints sulphuric acid .

7-8 am Visit mass grave of YTS lads I used to train with

8-10am Two hours on Kevin Ratcliffes head and football recognition charts.

10-12am Kicking practice (punch bag)

12-12.01am Kicking practice (Football)

12.01 - 2.pm Soak hands, feet and forehead in vinegar

2-3pm Warm up and kick about exercises.

3-4.45 pm Keep dugout seat warm till suspension ends

4.45-4.50pm I'm sat on by Bobby and Don while the opposing team passes dugout and enters dressing room.

5-6pm Evening meal : Raw meat and a thigh bone to gnaw on.

6pm Chained up again in cage till next match day

Frank Gillender,
Rowlands Gill

Dear Editor

I wish to complain in the strongest possible terms. Who in their right mind arranged Hull City to be at a home game against the same night that Barry Manilow was played on 'in Town'?

As I lit my candle and watched my hero 'Bazza', belting out the old faves, I wondered what the outcome of the match would be. I was pleased that AFC Bournemouth won, but disappointed that I missed Luthers' four goal home debut.

There again, its not every night that it's possible to sing along with Barry is it?

Yours in tune

Dennis Young

Out Of Cou

LETTERS LETTERS

AUNTIE SOCIAL ANSWERS YOUR QUESTIONS.....

Dear Auntie Social,

Can you do anything to stop the screening of live soccer matches on TV? My husband watches all of them, saying "this will be a great game" and at the end he says "what a load of rubbish". Personally, I think the sport is pathetic - 22 grown men having nothing better to do than kicking a bag of wind around, dirtying their Persil white shorts and getting boozed-up in the pubs afterwards. I think he uses the matches as an excuse to get out of washing-up. There are about 3 weeks of dirty dishes in the sink, and I've totally ran out of clean crockery. Can he be cured? Please help!

Yours, In Vain,
Mrs. Mad Dog

Auntie Social says......I don't know about curing your husband Mrs Mad Dog, but isn't it about time you got your finger out and washed a few pots yourself? As for you husband it seems that he's suffering from what is termed the 'Brian Moore Syndrome', which leads sufferers to believe that each game gets better the longer it goes on, and leads you to constantly say "the only thing lacking is goals"! I suggest you "tempt" him away from the telly on a Sunday afternoon.....leave fourteen cans of TIGERCOLA near the dirty dishes !!!

Hull, Hell and Happiness

The Spur

GIVE US A T

Dear Give us a T,
I have always wondered, in all the sixty years that I have travelled to matches at White Hart Lane, what the 'Audere est Facere' motto from the club badge means?

B. Smith, E17

Mr Smith, if you don't know now, I am afraid that you never will. For the four hundred and fifty seventh time of asking 'Audere est Facere' is latin and translates as "Spurs fans are illiterate twats who didn't ever study latin. Signed the Chairman."

Dear Give us a T,
I am a materialistic Spurs supporter, who posesses nearly everything and any-thing you could possibly imagine collect-able in connection with this, our wonderful club.

My main field of interest lies in collecting all the match programmes. I have every home and away programme since the club were first formed in 1882 - except one. A friendly in Paris, on 1st March 1913, against Red Star Belgrade, which is quite worthless really. If anyone has a mint condition copy of this that they can spare, I'll exchange if for the last week's pro-gramme at home to Portsmouth, which, although it has the odd page missing, is a good copy.

Yours,
Mr C. White

P.S. Has anyone got the commerative silk tie from the 1961 FA Cup Final ?

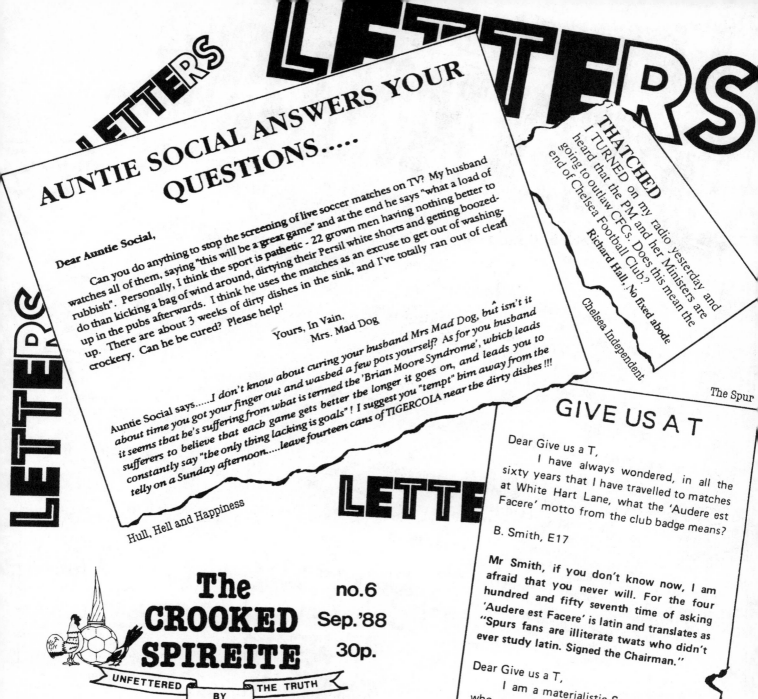

The CROOKED SPIREITE

no.6
Sep.'88
30p.

UNFETTERED BY THE TRUTH

It's Pinocchio!

At no time did we try to operate outside the League

We were always interested in what was best for football

GULP!

— BBC TELETEXT —

JULY 13th, 1986

Inside:
FULHAM FIX-
SCOTTISH CUP ○ FSA ○ EURO '88

MORE LIES! pp.4&5
the truth behind the slur: p.25

PLUS! all the usual rubbish.

LETTERS

THE CUSHION THROWER REPLIES.

All correspondence will probably be misquoted, and treated with the greatest disrespect, if it bears any resemblance to the load of old garbage we got in our first mail bag.

AND THE AIR TURNED BLUE.

Dear Blue Wail,
I thought your magazine wasn't bad but you could improve it alot by having a lot more swearing.

Brian Campbell, Crosby.

Fuck Off. **Ed.**

TRIVIAL PURSUITS.

Dear Blue Wail,
Just a note to say how much I enjoyed the mag. I must say that I wasn't too impressed with the quiz. Instead of testing peoples knowlege of trivia, why not test their imagination and offer a prize to the first person to come up with say, ten good things about the Simod Cup. Or perhaps name five advantages of supporting Manchester United ?.

John Baker, Runcorn.

The only good thing about the Simod Cup is that you don't have to queue to get into the matches. **Ed.**

Blue Wail

The Proclaimer

Dear Proclaimer,
I like to think of myself as a fair minded and reasonable football supporter, opposed to bigots and other mindless idiots who populate the football grounds across the country, albeit in small numbers. Tangible proof of my outlook on football is the fact that I buy many of the different club Fanzines although I'm a Hibbie through and through. It's good to get a view of the game in Scotland an indeed Britain as a whole. It's interesting to see that fans have many gripes in common.

The other week I bought Issue 4 of 'Follow, Follow' the Rangers Fanzine. Admittedly I was partly impelled to buy it after the amount of adverse publicity it had been given in other Fanzines. Sectarianism, bigotry, you know the sort of thing I mean. However I had also read that the editors of 'Follow, Follow' had made a concerted effort to improve the content so I picked up 'Follow, Follow' expecting to read a well balanced, informative and witty 'Fanzine which one might expect from a club which has a following the size of Rangers'. Instead I find *THE EDITOR!* writing such gems as "I personally don't think that songs celebrating the Battle of the Boyne or the Seige of Derry have got much to do with football but don't see how they could be looked upon as being offensive by anyone apart from (a) social workers, (b) IRA sympathisers, (c) anti-protestant bigots or (d) any combination of a, b or c."

How could anyone with any semblance of a brain write such insulting rubbish? Using the same analogy as the editor of 'Follow, Follow', the only people likely to be offended by racist remarks are:-
(a) social workers, (b) ANC sympathisers, (c) anyone with a different colour of skin to that of the originator of the remarks, (d) anti-white bigots or (e) any combination of a, b, c or d.
And that the only people likely to be offended by sexist remarks are:-
(a) social workers, (b) feminist sympathisers, (c) women or (d) any combination of a, b, or c.
Do the writers not realise that any person with a sense of decency or who cares about the dignity of their fellow human beings would be offended? Or have Rangers supporters been steeped in the bigotry of their own club for so long that they can't see these things.

M.R. GRY, PURLEY

LETTERS

Not The View

MAGIC

Dear NTV,

What is the magic of going to Celtic Park?

Is it being covered in muck at the bottom of Janefield Street or being stood on or shit on by a Constabulary horse?

Is it being pushed in and out of different queues by brainless stewards?

Maybe it is spending 50p on a programme to use as bog-paper once you've waded through six inches of urine and found that there's nothing to wipe your bum on in the toilets?

Is it spending almost £1 buying "hot" brown water and a cold pie with grease filling (yum yum!)?

Is it standing behind the fart-a-minute in the Jungle?

Is it missing the Celts' winning goal because a Polis has just stood in front of you?

No, the magic of going to Parkhead is seeing 40,000 malcontents being turned into 23,000. Not even Paul Daniels could do that!

Yours Contentedly

J McGINN
Glasgow.

Not The View

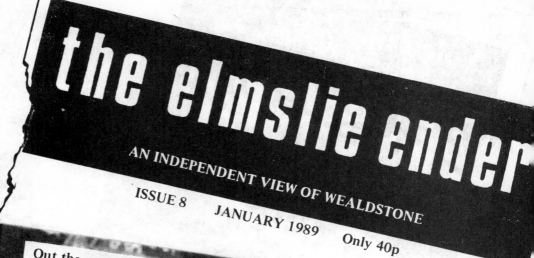

the elmslie ender

AN INDEPENDENT VIEW OF WEALDSTONE

ISSUE 8   JANUARY 1989   Only 40p

EAST FIFE v COWDENBEATH
Match Programme 25/2/89

An object lesson in how to reach a target market by effective advertising

The Wild Rover

Out the way everyone, it's that bloody round white thing again !

STILL WONDERING HOW WE GOT RELEGATED ?

AWAYDAY TO FAREHAM.......WEALDSTONE ON TV.......
......BEAZER CLUBCALL.......BARNET SIGN MARADONA!

BRITAINS MOST BANNED FOOTBALL MAGAZINE !

GUESS THE TOILET

No 11

VICTORY ISSUE - APRIL

Voice of The Valley
The INDEPENDENT Charlton mag

WE'RE ~~GOING~~

We're supposed

to be at

HOME!

The Spur

only bricks

and mortar?

AFC Bournemouth's
new yuppie stadium

1 Casino
2 Operatic Theatre
3 Overseas Properties Estate Agency
4 Swiss Bank
5 American Express Office
6 Real Tennis Court
7 Dry Ski Slope
8 Stock Brokers
9 Luxury Cruise Booking Agents
10 Porsche Showrooms
11 Rent a Jag - Limousine Rental
12 Helicopter Pad
13 Wine Bar
14 Game Bird Breeding Aviary
15 Indoor Clay Pigeon Shooting
16 Licensed Restaurant
17 Yachting Showroom
18 Racehorse Stud Farm

a Home Supporters Terracing
b Home Supporters Seating Area
c Away Supporters Terracing
d Directors Stand & Guest Bars
e Disabled Enclosure -
   unfortunately you can't see
   the pitch, but everyone
   keeps dry
f I D card Computer Control Room
g High Class Executive Boxes

1   18   17
2   d
    g
3   a
    g
    b
4   6   7
5   8   9   10

Out Of Court

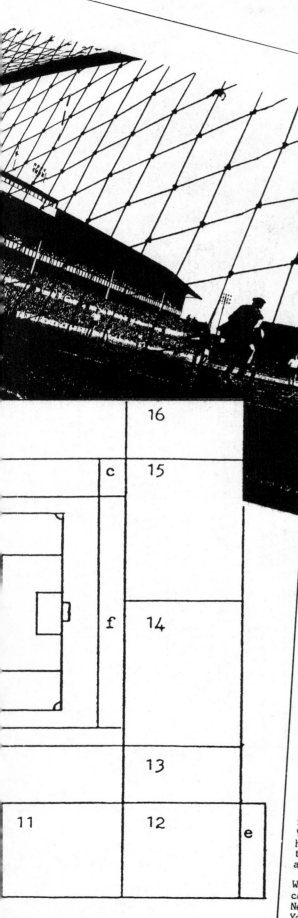

A NEW BRIDGE? BUT WHERE?

One person who hopes Chelsea lose the battle of The Bridge is me. I've been watching Chelsea since August 1964 and believe Im as well qualified to offer an opinion as anyone.

If Chelsea win their planning application and go ahead and redevelop The Bridge (again) it will be a big and costly mistake. To contemplate such a building programme in West London which could take 8 years to complete will bring local traffic to a standstill, and once the development is finished will bring misery to the thousands of fans trying to get to and from their beloved Bridge.

Chelsea as a board, as a club and as a group of supporters are keen to make the same mistake as Brian Mears and his band of men tried some 15 years ago.

Look at what is planned.

1. Use architects who aren't best qualified to design a modern stadium.
2. Give the go ahead for 3 more ugly stands.
3. Have the smallest pitch in the league.
4. Suffer pitch problems through high walling and poor ventilation.
5. Bulid it too small.
6. Not going in with someone else. (Ground share.)
7. Expect fans to pay yet again through discomfort and high prices.
8. Tolerate the boards choice rather than be given a questionnaire to fill in.
9. Lose out in the transfer market through lack of cash.
10. Cope with more years of lack of atmosphere.

The new proposal should be along the following lines.

1. Easy access - Chelsea's new home should be away from West London, out where the land is cheaper and where it is possible to build a major new road and rail links to the stadium.
2. Comfort and safety - Provide comfortable surroundings to attract people not currently attending football, and provide a safe arena for them to watch the game.
3. Ground share and pre-sell to off set costs - Build the new ground with another club. Palace are a club already sharing, they have potential so it makes sense for tomorrows ground to be shared by 2 clubs or more. Pre-sell executive boxes and other sponsered areas in a much bigger way than is currently in practice to raise building capital.
4. Large enough to attract semi-finals, and maybe a European league in the future. -Don't build it for todays needs, be confident and make a new market. Attract people who don't come to football instead of moaning about those who used to come. Make sure the new ground is large capacity.
5. Multi-use is not just every other Saturday - Incorporate other fund raising areas within the complex ie, conference suites, hotel, sports arenas, concerts. Infact anything that brings income into the stadium.
6. Designed by footballs leading architects - Use only footballs top architects, not necessarily from England, but people who are proven.
7. Bright and colourful seating - Make sure the ground is bright and welcoming, not just blue seats, blue posts, blue roofs etc etc. Create a pleasant atmosphere through colour.
8. No obstruction of view by fences - Arrange seating and security fencing in such a manner so as not to spoil the view of those at the front.
9. Extensive use of private security firms - Use private security firms instead of a heavy police prescence. Police are unwelcome at football grounds, they create more problems than solve them. Rid them of an easy afternoons overtime and provide security firms with the job. They help to maintain a friendlier atmosphere.
10. Still called Stamford Bridge - Any new ground we would be proud to call home. Call it STAMFORD BRIDGE.

Losing your home is never the end of the world and if Chelsea leave Fulham Road things can only get better.

The area is not suitable for a modern stadium for one major reason - CAR PARKING!
90% of our journeys are by car. To work, shopping, visiting, holidays, leisure time etc. That accepted it seems incredible that so much money is to be invested in a new football ground and nobody can drive to it.

Wake up Chelsea, build a new ground people can get to in comfort, watch football in comfort and then get home in comfort. Next year is 1990, don't build a stadium in the same place. You won't attract new supporters, you'll lose more of your existing ones.

The Red Card

FANS

BLUE HORIZON

The weather was good as the four of us set off for St. Andrews. About halfway there the fog came down. Visions of the game being called off were soon dispelled as we reached sunny Birmingham. With the floodlights in sight we pulled into the pub car park and hurriedly entered the building with eager anticipation. Our horror as we were served freezing cold lager in plastic receptacles was plain to see. We stuck out like a skillful, sporting player would in a Portsmouth team. A sea of faces all with whining Birmingham accents seemed to stare at us as we tried to blend in with the surroundings.

We somehow managed to escape without mishap from a pub that was as friendly as a crocodile with toothache. Onwards we drove to another boozer, nearer the away end of the ground. The area surrounding St. Andrews really is from another world. Acres of desolate waste ground strewn with a confetti consisting of cans, bottles, and a mountain of litter, are a stark contrast to the pleasant tree-lined approaches to Dean Court.

As we parked in the street and got out of the car, a young lad of about 10 asked our driver Eddie (for it is he) "Look after your car for a quid mister"? into the pub and we noticed our car and the road outside were displayed on a video screen above the door. When asked what was the purpose of the security camera, a Brum supporter told us that the landlord had recently been shot in the road. I half expected to see the Kray twins walk by.

Further conversation with several Blues fans revealed that the St. Andrews faithful did not hold Carl Richards in the same vein as Pele. It's a shame that things have turned sour for 'Bruno', because he is a nice genuine lad. The Blues tell us that they are looking forward to their first double of the season while we are looking for revenge. A good friendly drink. I just wish the mass media would inform the public of the many amiable encounters that were happening, on the same time that

Saturday lunchtime, all over England. But I expect the few moronic macho men who want to do battle, will be the only fans whose behaviour is sensational enough to be reported.

On to the ground and a crowd of just under 6,500 (larger than Wimbledon V Aston Villa) barely scratches the surface of St. Andrews. A fine turnout of Bournemouth fans though and all prepared to shout and cheer the lads to victory. Birminghams' fans seemed to accept that it would be a depressing afternoon. From the first whistle, the only thing they thought worth shouting was 'Pendry Out!'. In all fairness their team did put in a terrible performance and relegation looks inevitable. To cap it all, it started to rain in the first half.

Sean Teale had a cracking debut in an otherwise uneventful first 45 minutes. Half time and a chance to visit the jewel in the crown. Birminghams' open air super loo! We complain about our own South End toilets, but at least you're under a roof when you're doing the business. And it was still raining.

The second half. An instant Mark Newson goal and the Cherries cruise to a 1-0 away win. Back to the car where the young lad is moving faster than Luther Blissett, scampering up and down the line of vehicles, collecting his fee from people who promised to pay him after the game. The journey home and another league ground visited. One that will undoubtedly play host to a 3rd Division team next season. On reflection, it is a strange experience to see a good ground, such as St. Andrews, only a quarter full. I feel that our little Dean Court ground has a much greater scope for creating a better atmosphere than many other grounds. It's all down to the fans.

Postman Pat.

Out Of Court

A St Johnstone fan enjoys a typically erotic dream.

TIL DEATH DO US PART?

Life after Charlton? Richard Wiseman struggles to cope with the inconceivable.

There was a feature in the Independent Magazine a few weeks ago by the novelist David Lodge about his boyhood hero, Charlie Vaughan. The article extols the virtues of Sam Bartram, Chris Duffy and Vaughan and describes how the author listened to the 1946 Cup Final in tears. But, for me, the most amazing part is the following sentence:

"...my emotions were largely invested in a professional football team, Charlton Athletic, which I supported from 1946, when I was 11, 'til about 1951, when my leisure interests turned towards the arts, and girls."

This casual admission leaves me stunned. What is all this about leisure interests turning elsewhere? And since when has supporting Charlton been leisure? Is this man trying to tell me you can grow out of supporting Charlton?

Ever since I was first taken down Lansdowne Road on Boxing Day 1961 to see Charlton (bottom of Division 2) beat Sunderland (with Brian Clough at centre-forward) 2-0, I have assumed that I am suffering from a lifelong affliction. I clamoured all week to be taken to the next match (FA Cup Third Round v Scunthorpe) and eventually got my way. 27 years, two relegations, three promotions, nine managers and one Danish international later I'm still there, wide-eyed and red-scarfed, every Saturday. It has never occurred to me that maturity might offer other avenues to pleasure. For me, it's a life sentence.

There have only been two occasions when I thought I might become an ex-Charlton supporter. The first was after a pre-season friendly with Millwall in the early 1970s. As I left the ground my right eye came into painfully close contact with a hairy Deptford fist, and I remember that every game I'd ever seen flashed past my eyes before I hit the pavement.

I survived, however, and it wasn't until March 1984, when daily bulletins were being issued about the club's demise, that I contemplated bereavement again. It is with great shame that I admit leaving the bedside vigil for a skiiing holiday in Austria, where I spent an outrageous sum on a Sunday paper which informed me that the Blackburn game hadn't been played.

As far as I was concerned that meant liquidation and I was faced with the awesome prospect of finding something else to fill the emotional Saturday afternoon void. The arts? Girls? Leyton Orient? It was too much to contemplate. Once again, of course, reprieve was granted.

I suppose the departure from The Valley might have offered a third opportunity to retire from active supportership, but, after 25 years through thin and thin, there was little chance of my kicking the habit with the land of milk and Lenny just round the corner.

No, I'm resigned to it - I'll be supporting Charlton until that last great unavoidable tackle arrives.

But why should it stop then? I've often wondered what twenty to five might be like in Heaven. I picture a giant celestial vidiprinter spelling out scores like Arsenal 0 Charlton 7 (seven). A cherubic Desmond Lynam commenting: "That means Charlton maintain their fifteen point lead over Liverpool, and with the two teams meeting at The Valley next week the championship could be staying in SE7 for yet another season."

And Hell? Hell is a giant Selhurst Park in which Charlton are playing Crystal Palace in a home Fourth Division relegation match. The score is 0-0 until the 89th minute when Palace bring on their substitute, recently purchased from Manchester United. He beats eleven men to score the winner. It is Ralph Milne. All the 75 buses are cancelled. It's raining.

And yet, back among the living, David Lodge can calmly announce that supporting Charlton was just a phase he went through. Is this normal? Is it healthy growth? Of course it isn't! The man is clearly suffering from arrested development, an inability to form anything but the most superficial relationships, an immature personality and emotional bankruptcy. If he can't exhibit a full-size pathological obsession for Charlton Athletic by his age then he's clearly a social deviant.

Five thousand Selhurst sufferers can't be mad.

Voice of the Valley

```
GO   WITH   GARSON
GO   WITH   GARSON
GO   WITH   GARSON
```

1. METHILated Spirits

Ah, the magic of the Scottish Cup. There we were at the pulsating bus station in Edinburgh eagerly anticipating a pulsating, end to end fever pitched cup tie at Methil...but first getting there.

This was the day I found out that Methil is a bugger to get to if you don't have a motor. The nearest train station is in Kirkcaldy, so that meant getting the bus.

The Fife Coastliner(sounds ominous ,eh) was waiting at the stance looking as sumptuosly comfortable as all the other "Scottish bus group" buses. You know the sort..no room for your legs, design of the seat gives you a sore neck, and of course its either freezing or steaming hot.

£3 for a day return, not bad, then I asked the driver how long it would take. Two hours he said with a half way grin, two-ferking-hours,Christ it's twenty minutes or something by car. Still this is what Saturdays all about.

So we set off Daily Record in hand to read the team news, "Airdrie will be unchanged" they say as usual. That must be about the 25th week running(what splendid football coverage). Everything was fine until we got into Fife. We made the mistake of sitting upstairs-it was more like being on a boat than a bus. And of course it went through all those small towns-Burntisland,Inverkeithing,Kinghorn ad infinitum. Gradually we began to notice a distinct lack of Rangers buses in the same vicinity. They were due to be playing Raith. This was perhaps due to the monsoon(which did not enhance the "scenery")

As we pulled (literally) into Kirkcaldy panic set in as the Raith game was off, oh shit we're not going all this way for it to be off. An eternity lasting twenty minutes elapsed before Methil was reached and it was a relief to get off that bus.

The first thing to do was check if it was on-yes..joy overcame us-next stop pie then the pub. The pie was disgusting,you could actually pour the grease out. The pub was superbly placed(?)-right beside Bayview. The usual reception of staring locals was had on entering. The biggest surprise was the jukebox..a tasteful mix of Kenny Rogers, The Clash and The Undertones, pretty diverse.

This was my first time at Bayview and a ground with less character would be difficult to find. The only interesting feature was the view of the oil rig platform being built at the docks. After all the trials and tribulations of the day the game sort of passed me by. I think the thought of the return trip contributed. A 2-1 win was had and as it turned out Dundee UTD awaited.

After the game it was back to the pub to check the coupons. Peter(my colleague here at OTL)only needed Clyde to beat Cowdenbeath for £16, but of course it was a draw,which as it happened was quite painless as we were just summed up the day. The return journey ,as it happened was quite painless as we were both knackered and fell asleep. What a day ,but thats the magic of the cup.
....

NEXT ISSUE: Inverness or bust
FORTHCOMING ATTRACTIONS: Spewing up on the train to Berwick,
The shows at Cowdenbeath,
The Orchard Hotel in Falkirk   bet you can't wait

Only The Lonely

FANS

ARE YEOVIL GOING DOWNHILL ?

We Visited The Famous Huish Slope

BELOW: An optician's eye test chart for the referee of the Boston v. Yeovil game.

For the lengthy journey west to Yeovil it was one of those old fashion summer days that belong firmly to the past - hot, warm and a sunwashed countryside as the train rattled like it was trying to shake itself loose, as we travelled through what was usually England's grey and pleasant (Get to the bit about the football and dispense with the descriptions - you expect a Booker prize for a fanzine -Ed) land. (Thank you - Ed).

Warnings, though, are hereby givenout to all prospective supporters who want to add Yeovil's Huish to the their list of grounds visited. The train takes two and a half hours to reach "Yeovil" and then stops in the proverbial middle of nowhere called Yeovil Junction - perhaps best described by thinking about one of those Apollo photos of the moon. From here it is another ten minute bus journey into town. At least they built the ground exceptionally nearthe town centre, inspite of its 1 in 2 slope running across the pitch. Referring to the match itself will not take too long; basically Boston had more shots that missed than a weekend Clay Pigeon shoot. With perfectly applied irony, when the Pilgrims did score it was such a piece of bad luck for the Yeovil defender and goalkeeper that they both must have expected to be hit by a piece of falling space junk that afternoon their luck was so bad.

Luck is a good friend but a horrible enemy, and going into the last five minutes defending the customary one goal lead saw Boston lose the three points with two minutes to go. A hard cross from the left hit Cusack point blank on the arm before he could get himself out of the way, and the referee thought he'd like to see another goal before his long drive home, so a penalty was duely awarded and converted.

We filtered out as the sun was going in as a protest, and were left to ponder at least two thoughts on the enormous journey home: 1- Why is Yeovil at least six days journey by pack mule from Yeovil station, and 2- Why call it Yeovil station when it's nowhere near it; Euston isn't called Liverpool Central or Pontefract.

IF A MAN HANDLES UNINTENTIONALLY
THEN IT IS MOST DEFINITELY NOT A PENALTY

From Behind Your Fences

SUNDAY JANUARY 8th
PORT VALE (1) 1 V NORWICH (0) 3
SCORER: WEBB
VALE: - GREW, WEBB, HUGHES, WALKER, HAZEL, SPROSON, MILLS, EARLE, FUTCHER (GRIM)
       BECKFORD, RILEY (ACE)
NORWICH: - WHO CARES! But unfortunately Townsend!

Another day of FA Cup giant-killing was in store. Norwich, leaders of the first division (somehow) since early September, travelling to play the valiant wizards ("the only cultured footballing side in Division 3" - Peter Jones BBC Radio Sport 8.1.89) conquerors of Tottenham (who?) the previous season.

But, would the Vale be overwhelmed by the huge support (only come in a taxi) which would undoubteably arrive from the first division high flyers. Not a bit. The first half was totally according to plan-Vale domination from the off. "Which is the first division side? Who is the team playing all in red? Has anybody found my, glasses?" One spectator was heard to say.

And then.... the magical moment. The occurence with the regularity of Haleys Comet - An Alan Webb goal!! A crowded goalmouth, ascrambled clearance, and there's Webby, thundering an unstoppable right footer past Gunn 1-0 to the Vale and no more than they deserved.

The second half followed the same pattern - more Vale domination. Corner after corner from the home side (well two anyway). Then the turning point : Futcher is through but blatantly pulled by the no 5 - a penalty surely... Referee glances towards the Norwich Manager who is in a perfect position to see, the unbiased verdict No penalty!

Then Norwich played better and won 3-1

MAN OF THE MATCH; DAVID RILEY

The Memoirs of Seth Bottomley

BLOW-UP!
INFLATION HITS THE LEAGUE

IN an otherwise dull season, one of the best things that could have happened is the rise of the inflatable. As everyone knows by now, Man City can take credit for bringing a smile back to the game.

Maine Road went bananas after fans transformed Imre Varadi's name into Imre Banana. Whether this was in honour of the size of his dick, his ability to bend the ball, or that they couldn't pronounce his name remains unclear, but a few bunches of inflatable Fyfes later, football had a full scale craze on its hands.

The sight of Grimsby fans bouncing up and down with hundreds of haddock after they'd scored in the FA Cup must have even brought a smile to a miserable bastard like Colin Whineyhan. Then again, he was probably sitting there wondering whether the fish should be exempt from carrying ID cards. The point is, that the sight of something as stupid as that reminds everyone that going to a game can still be a laugh (well, for some fans, anyway).

The terraces are alive and not kicking, Harry the Haddock is a celebrity and suddenly people believe football can be fun again.

Rex International, the firm who sell the things can't believe their luck. Since the haddock and the bananas we've seen fried eggs, alligators, gorillas and skeletons appear around the country. Wigan Athletic have adopted baked bean tins, Leicester have gone for dinosaurs, and Derby County for black puddings. Forest even went as far as to have the club logo printed on their bananas.

Inflatables finally reached Upton Park in the rather obvious shape of hammers, though the ground has yet to be transformed into a mass open-air woodwork class. It has to be said they're pathetic pink claw hammers, though there are some more appropriate wobbly sledgehammers in evidence. A quick glance through the Rex catalogue also reveals that they sell blow up Santas and lifeboats, either of which would suit our position more.

What of our neighbours? Well Spurs fans might appreciate some blow up wallets or inflatable bagels, but they don't make those either, so they'll have to make do with champagne bottles.

Arsenal, showing the good nature that readily endears them to all, banned inflatables for a while. Nevertheless it should be remembered that it was Arsenal fans who produced blow up sex dolls in '87 for a Tottenham game after David Pleat's indiscretions were revealed. Since the ban was lifted Gunners fans might like to invest in some inflatable donkeys in honour of their captain, or maybe some arms to raise aloft to bolster their frequent appeals for offside.

Luton might like some fans, and Charlton could do with an inflatable ground till they move back.

Personally, we'd like to see the North Bank full of pink flamingos — just for the hell of it. Still anything's better than watching another bloody condom floating around.

Interesting People

As a new idea, for the Lion Roars, I thought what better than to write about the many types of interesting people you meet when travelling to Millwall away games, be it by train, private car, horse drawn barge or any other form of transport.

To avoid mentioning any names, I will start this article off by referring to people, I have come across, travelling to away games by British Rail, under the category they relate to.

First of all, that most non perverse person: THE TRAIN SPOTTER. This most intriguing of characters, can be found on main line railway stations, all hours of the day and night, whilst travelling to away games at the most exotic of destinations. The Bible of a train spotter, is The Motive Power, available at most mainline station newsagents. From this the objective arises to gain the number of every type of locomotive or unit train in the country. It is indeed a strange phenomenon that most of these people when they are not bespectacled or puss infected, bear an uncanny resemblance to either Paul Hinshelwood or Les Briley. They can be seen either taking Photographs of all the types of trains, however characterless, making tape recordings of the power, or in many cases, applauding the poetry in motion whilst a train leaves the station.

Whilst myself being satisfied following Millwall the length and breadth of the country, in stark contrast, THE SOCCER PERVERT can be found not just being content with visiting the 92 League clubs, but travelling long distances to places as exclusive as Cleator Moor Celtic, Glasshoughton Welfare or Wooton Basset Town. Armed with a copy of the Non League Directory, known conversations for these Roy Orbison lookalikes are such topics as the previous weeks line up for Hounslow in the Westgate Insurance Cup, or with the customary phlegm distributed all around, the mention of Bashley's giantkilling feats. In the FA Vase. Needless to say all such conversations are loud enough for the whole carriage to savour.

An away trip for THE DRUNKEN IDIOT, generally starts very early, before British Rail would consider it feasible to make the trains devoid of alcohol, and concerns the consistent inebriation of one such person from normality to being pissed by the consuming of British Rail packs of four, throughout the journeys duration. The drunkard can be the scourge of the soccer pervert; both intimidating and interrupting their fascinating discussions with manic outbursts and general behaviour of this type of individual revolves around farting loudly or in some cases lying on a seat cushion in the position of a Buxted chicken, and igniting ones farts as they occur. These are just three types of interesting people you will come across on away trips, I'm sure there are more?

WINSTON KODOGO

ATTACK, ATTACK, ATTACK

CLWYD LGE.—Prem Div: Mostyn 3, Mold Alex 2,000 — Rhyl Victory Club 2, Pilkingtons 1 — Sealand Rovers 1, Hawarden Rangers 2.

"Sunday Telegraph"

In these days of defence orientated tactics, it is particularly pleasing to see Mold Alex continue to push forward when they were 1,500-nil up, and refuse to substitute a forward with a defender and sit back and attempt to consolidate their lead. Not surprisingly, with all this attacking going on, the home side did manage to catch Alex on the break three times.

Blue Wail

TO HELL... AND BACK
Soaking wet in Newport...

12.30pm: Leave Kidder.

1.20pm: Go past sign on M50 saying "Welcome To Wales" — a contradiction in terms if ever there was one. Sign raises healthy chorus of "What a load of bollocks" in car.

1.40pm: Getting thirsty. Eventually turn off road towards what looks like pleasant pub. Drive into car par and walk round to front. Shit, it's a motel and a plastic-looking one at that. Return to car.

1.41pm: Owner of motel walks directly behind reversing Harriers fans and knocks

The Soup

on car window. "What's your problem?", he demands menacingly. We say we haven't got one thank you but he has. Firstly his motel's crap and secondly he's living in Wales. Drive off. One-nil.

1.50pm: Starts raining.

1.59pm: Arrive in Newport. Good grief. If Wales ever gets piles, this is where they'll be. It's like Bilston without the scenery.

2.00pm: Go into grotty pub near ground. Bloody keg beer. Is it not possible to buy a pint of proper beer in this excuse

for a country? Settle for Newcastle Brown and Guinness. Talk to some pleasant old codgers who are Newport fans. They go on about "the glory days" and letting John Aldridge go for practically nothing a few years ago. I tell them they're likely to have even more to moan about by 4.45pm today.

2.40pm: Leave grotty pub and walk to ground. Absolutely pissing down. Somerton Park is next to a mass of railway lines and possibly one of the vilest grounds on the planet. If a bomb fell on it, it could do up to £1.75 worth of damage.

2.50pm: Due to inclement nature of elements, forsake standing up on terraces for seat in stand next to dreaded Brouwer Bros (hereinafter known as Bros). Apart from directors about five rows behind, we appear to be the only Harriers fans in the stand. A few hundred are behind the goal though and in good voice. Both Macca getting soaked. I offer him my brolly, which he bravely declines. What a man.

3pm: Peeeeep! Come on you Reds...

3.10pm: Looking good. Harriers off to promising start.

3.24pm: Oh joy! Micky Tuohy crosses for Ocker to turn his marker and bang home from 12 yards. One up and completely in control despite rain, which is threatening to turn game into scene from The Cruel Sea.

Did You Know :   That the Scilly Isles only have two football teams, who play each other every week ? In the English First Division there is, of course, only one football team who play one of 19 teams there to make up the numbers every week.

Storming With Menace

For me, the love affair with those red and white stripes started unpromisingly on a cold midweek night around 25 years ago when an undistinguished United team stumbled to a 1-0 Division One defeat against a Blackpool side inspired by a young red-haired inside-forward called Alan Ball.

I was still at junior school and bitterly envious of the ball-boys who had what seemed the glamorous task of scurrying across the huge cricket pitch to retrieve some wildly mishit clearance or hopelessly sliced pass.

My huge family, Wednesdayites almost to a man or woman, soon started to spread out from Attercliffe and I ended up far from Sheffield, in the Cheshire commuter belt at a school where one thing stopped Manchester United and City supporters beating each other up: the chance to beat up someone who had the audacity to support Sheffield United.

Being on the receiving end of the occasional dose of grievous bodily harm I could stand, however; other disappointments were much harder to take: the departures of Jones and Birchenall, Currie and Salmons (but not, please God, Agana and Deane), watching a very good side break up in the early 1970s instead of perhaps becoming a great one, the bitter taste of relegation, seeing players who did nothing for United play like men inspired after being transferred, while those who stayed showed no evidence of commitment to the club or the supporters, the pitiful inability to put together any kind of cup run.....

above all, the sheer frustration of seeing Liverpool, Manchester, and other outposts enjoy success while the home of football remained a second-class soccer city, with United eventually slumping to the very rock-bottom.

As Flashing Blade readers know, however, failure to win trophies, or even many matches, does not dampen the ardour of a true fan. Nor, in my case, does working in London and living in Kent, entailing 400-mile round trips to enjoy such delights as a 1-1 draw against Hartlepool or the worst match I've ever witnessed, the unbelievably inept FA Cup fiasco against Fulham a couple of years ago in which both teams should have been disqualified for inflicting pain on the public.

There are many happy memories, of course. Younger Unitedites must be getting sick of hearing about things that happened when they were still in their prams, but the night of that Cardiff match in 1971....going to Old Trafford with my team, yes Sheffield United, as the best in the land, only beaten by a unique piece of sheer genius....Woody hitting four as we stuck seven past Ipswich....the great TC sitting on the ball in a moment of marvellous arrogance during the thrashing of Arsenal....More recently: the clinical striking of Keith Edwards....a great night against Liverpool....two promotions....and now, of course, Dave Bassett and the first genuine hope for many years of good times to come.

I took my sons Oliver and Dominic, aged seven and barely six, to their first United game at Gillingham last year and watched in disbelief as the eleven men in red and white stripes played with more passion and commitment than I have ever seen from a United team. The result, the travesty of a 2-1 defeat, hardly seemed to matter - certainly not to my boys, who immediately joined the Junior Blades and began demanding Saturday trips to Bramall Lane and pictures of Deano and Tony to put on their walls. The United supporters, who immediately joined the Junior Blades and began demanding Saturday trips to Norwich, a little sad but full of pride. The United support-

We have just returned from Norwich, a little sad but full of pride. The United support-ers were incredible: thousands of us singing, cheering and sharing the whole range of emotions from jubilation to despair in a matter of minutes, joined by bonds of tradition, heritage and just plain stubbornness, to the club and city we love, bonds among football fans which Margaret Thatcher - miserably suspicious of any grouping bar those founded on wealth and greed - can never understand and so wants to smash.

My love affair lives on, and for my boys, a new generation, it has just begun.

DAVID MARSH, TUNBRIDGE WELLS, KENT.

Flashing Blade

FANS

Am I Blue?

3.45pm: Peep! Half-time. Even the bogs are in the open, which poses problem as you have to hold brolly with one hand and willy in the other. Hope I don't get confused.

3.46pm: Blag way into social club, which is horrible. Nasty beer, nasty furniture, nasty accents.

3.56pm: Peep! Come on you Reds.

3.58pm: Newport's Thompson booked after shocking tackle on Peter Howell, diving in over the top with both feet. Howell lucky to escape with leg still in one piece. We suggest ref sends Mr Thompson for early bath. He bottles it and just books him instead.

4.06pm: Disaster. The gochs get an equaliser after Harriers get caught at the back. Rain gets even heavier. Women and children to the lifeboats.

4.10pm: Looking grim. Welsh looking very dangerous. Bloke in far stand starts leading animals onto ark.

4.30pm: Welsh still on top this half, but we are defending well and continue plugging away. Allner should bring on Torville and Dean in these conditions, but

he opts for Rob Jones instead, who replaces Mark Dearlove. We give surrounding Newport fans rousing two bar chorus of Come On You Reds.

4.39pm: GOAL! Peter Howell and Jon Pearson, who's struggled for pace today, combine in nice move down the right. Pearson sends over great cross and Ocker rises from the waves like a Trident missile to nod it in. Back in front with two minutes to go. Newport fans very pissed off as celebrations get underway.

4.40pm: Come on ref!

4.41pm: Peep! Get in! Three vital points. God bless Ocker, Harriers and St George!

4.42pm: Blag way into Newport VP's Club. Have to buy Bros another bloody round. Offer them lift home to Cheltenham. They refuse on grounds they get free fish and chips on players' coach. SCANDAL.

4.43pm: Des Lynham, perhaps the greatest living human, with teleprinter results. Kettering only draw which means we are six points clear at the top. Big cheer from large Harriers contingent.

5.20pm: Leave club. Still pissing down. Wave to John the Harriers kit boy as he is swept away on 12 foot tidal wave, still pluckily hanging on to large wicker basket.

5.30pm: Reach car. Up periscope. Next stop Kiddy.

7pm: Kiddy. Pop into Aggborough for pint, gloat and read of somebody else's Argus. Win has gone to chairman Reynolds' head. He buys travelling Soup editorial team a beer. Cheers.

7.40pm: Indian takeaway to start victory celebrations.

9pm: Pub. More gloating, post-match analysis and lots of beer. The end of another perfect day.

When I wrote in issue 21 of CITY GENT of the trials and tribulations of being an Evertonian in Bradford I was concerned more with Liverpool's continued success than Bradford City. True, I did refer to the Bantam's emphatic 3-0 Cup victory over Everton in 1960, and I have been reminded of that match from time to time. It was, however, a long time ago, and very few Bradfordians under the age of forty could have witnessed that game. When I submitted my pre-season piece I had no idea that history was to repeat itself so soon.

Men and women with the curious title of Party Whips are the disciplinarians of Back Bench members of parliament, aand indeed of local councillors. It is their job to ensure that the maximum voting fodder is delivered on time to the Division Lobbies. Conservative Whips will certainly be attempting soon to dragoon their members, many reluctant, into voting for the Football Supporters Bill and its ludicrous membership scheme. Back in the 1960s when I was a Liverpool City councillor, the respective party whips could be relied upon to contrive an early finish when council meetings coincided with an Everton or Liverpool evening game. It is not so in Westminster; even a cup-tie is considered insufficient grounds for missing a vote. I was therefore in Westminster, two hundred miles away, when the fateful action took place at Valley Parade.

I share a tiny, claustrophobic office in parliament with a Glasgow colleague who has kindly provided a small combined TV and radio set. Radio 2 was therefore my contact with the match, never for me a pleasant listening experience. I wonder how other fans feel about radio commentaries? The tone of the commentator's voice invariably seems to indicate that Everton's opponents are on top. Each time they cross the half-way line a goal seems imminent, our attacks just disappear, and that is when we win 4-0!

When I turned on the radio we were already two down, but having listened to the half-time summary and the tale of early missed chances I was still convinced we would at least force a replay. Colin Harvey would be reading the riot act in the dressing room; hope springs eternal! When the third goal went in even my eternal optimism was dashed. If the radio had not been my colleague's it would have gone through the window, if only we had a window.

My office has its compliment of files, reference books and lists. It also reflects my political and personal interests, with political, football and jazz posters. My Everton calendar and team photographs, a cutting from the pre-Murdoch "Times" showing that Everton have won more games, collected more points and scored more goals than any other team in the history of the First Division. There is even an excerpt from a Neil Kinnoch speech on "Socialist Nationalisation" from the days when he also was a left wing socialist. There are posters celebrating the 15th year anniversary of Mal Webb's "Famous New Orleans Jazz Band"'s Monday night session at The Brown Cow, Bingley. No 1 on the list of numbers played on that pleasant occasion was an old New Orleans standard, "Am I Blue" - I certainly was.

When I returned to my office the following morning, my Everton calendar and list of Goodison Park Box Office Telephone Numbers had fallen off the wall. The fastening had come off the corner of my Trotsky poster and even he had turned his face to the wall. Returning to Bradford was worse; numerous individuals suddenly wishing to discuss nothing but football; a spirited chorus of "You're Not Going To Wembley" in the local; and the chairman of my constituency offering me a plastic ball autographed by City's three scorers.

Sadly, Everton were followed by Bristol City and Spurs by Hull, just as Dolan has been followed by Yorath. Yet nothing can take away these famous victories for the team, the manager and the fans. Did not a team, apparently without strikers, become the first to score three goals past Neville Southall this season? For my part I will have to live with the result for a long time yet. AM I BLUE!?

- PAT WALL (Bradford MP and Toffeeman)

FANS

MIKE LYONS TURNED MY SON INTO AN OLIVE

Okay, which bastard put Super Glue on my fingers?

THE AWAY DAY TO CHELTENHAM

Arriving at Cheltenham, the first impression offered to the visitor is just how much of an obviously prosperous and well to do area this is. Indeed, an inner-city riot in Cheltenham would no doubt involve locals lobbing petrol bombs at the police made out of empty Moet '68 bottles.

As always with football grounds, Whaddon Road was located at completely the opposite side of town from the station. However, the long walk was worth it, inspite of the defeat, due mainly to the goal which Glen Beech scored, which was worth walking a thousand miles barefooted through catcus fields to see.

When Beech received the ball 35 yards out and started the motions of attempting a volley bicycle kick, we were wandering who was going to retrieve the ball from the gardens behind the goal. Suddenly the Cheltenham goalkeeper stood stunned by the sonic boom which shook Gloucestershire to signal the velocity of Beech's shot going through the sound barrier, and entering the top corner of the net like a tank shell.

Sadly this was to provide the only real high spot, with Chris Cook and Stewart Hamill wasting several good chances. After equalising in injury time of the first half, Cheltenham prompty scored two more in injury in the second-half to clinch the meeting 3-1. At least the Cheltenham central defender, with the unpronouncable name, was considerably more restrained in his behaviour than for the league meeting at York Street a few weeks earlier, when he was considerably lucky to finish the match still a free man.

Apart from the impressive main stand, which runs approximately half the way along one side with seating for 1,200 people and provides covered terracing in front, the rest of the Whaddon Road ground is disappointing. There is nothing to speak of behind either goal, and the covered terracing along one side is so low you have to duck to watch the game, while the ball isn't being retrieved by an army of ballboys who sprint into action everytime the ball sails behind this bus stop-like structure.

For such a prosperous town which Cheltenham can justifiably lay claim to be, it was surprising to arrive at the ground to see that one untrusting local had left his bicycle chained to some railings, with one lock for the front wheel to the railings, another lock for the back wheel, and yet another lock for the main frame. I was going to nick his bell, but then I remembered that I'm not like that.

Finally, a hello to the Tranmere Rovers fans we met on the train, all of whom were enthusiastically telling us about their membership of TRASH (Tranmere Rovers Away in Silly Hats).

From Behind Your Fences

Motson Speak

Don't you just HATE some of the rubbish football commentators spout these days, ie. meaningless things like "getting a result". Losing 64-0 is STILL a result isn't it? The recent European Championships brought us some great football but sadly this was not matched by the accompanying commentaries, most of which deteriorated the more apparent it became that England fans who had booked for a second week in Germany would not be watching their own team in the latter stages. Below we list a compilation, complete with the real meaning, of some of the empty phrases employed by Motson & Co.

1. It's an absorbing contest —— It's crap!
2. It's a bit cat and mouse —— It's crap!
3. It could even go to penalties —— It's crap!
4. It's a contrast of styles —— It's crap!
5. It's a cautious start —— It's crap!
6. It's a bit tentative —— It's crap!
7. The defences are on top —— It's crap!
8. The pace has slowed a little —— It's crap!
9. Possibly time for substitutions —— It's crap!
10. It's crap! —— England are down 3-1

LOOKS LIKE WE CRACKED THE HOOLIGAN PROBLEM COLIN!

Fortune's
ALWAYS HIDING

A RIGHT ROYAL KNEES-UP FOR CHIRPY COCKNEYS EVERYWHERE

50p

12TH NOV 1991

WIN A BILLION IN BINGO

THE SPOTE
NOV 1991

WEST HAM CRASH TO BOTTOM OF 3RD.

LYALL SPEAKS
BLAH QUALITY PLAYERS
BLAH NO PANIC BLAH
RIGHT PLAYERS EIGHT
PRICE BLAH BLAH
BAD SUPPORTERS.
BLAH STILL IN
THE CUP BLAH

THE Scum

ATTENDANCES SLUMP AS I.D. CARDS BITE
ANOTHER SEVEN CLUBS BANKRUPT

INCE STRIKES AGAIN AS LIVERPOOL GO TOP

A DREAM OF LEICESTER
a poem by George Wood

I leant upon a wooden post
Surveying the scene afore my eyes
Of Leicester giving up the ghost
At goals by Pennyfather and from Wright

Leicester two, Palace four
From Filbert Street came the score
And Palace fans began to brag
For three more points were in the bag

I spied a Greenfinch on the stand
Such a pretty bird made me feel grand
Then came a through ball into space
I got there first to win the race

I sliced it to a Leicester man
Who tucked it home I felt so sad
And then another Leicester score
Tied it all up at four - four

George you prat
The fans all called
You're fat and senile
And you're bald

My blunder it had cost us dear
As I wallowed in my own self pity
It was the reason that I fear
They let me go to Cardiff City.

TONY MATTHEWS.

Eagle Eye

Living on the lifeline

Living on the lifeline

Croydon.
The Fairfield Halls.
Launch night of the Crystal Palace Lifeline Club.
Individual invites to a "very special evening" had been dropped through our doors.
Rumours were rife.
The "South London Press" speculated that CPFC were going public - selling shares in the club on the Stock Exchange. Like Spurs. No way ! Wouldnt touch 'em with a bargepole.
Met my mate in the foyer. Straight from work. Hungry. Thirsty. Went for a beer.
Familiar faces in the bar. Some of the first team looking sheepish in their club suits.
Smart blazers. Embarrassed looks. Nervous shuffles. Anxious glances. Eyes on watches.
Glossy leaflets. Stalls for holidays and Lada cars.
Snatches of conversation. "Whats all this about then ?". "Dunno".
Stewards in club ties usher us into the hall. Nice place. Good seats. Free. So what's the catch ? Money. Theyre after our money. No way ! Definitely not ! They can forget it. We pay enough to get into the poxy ground and watch a match from the drafty stand.
Not to mention the expensively thin programme.
No - they could have our support, moral, vocal or otherwise.
But if they asked for money they could get stuffed.
Around us we heard similar declarations. The expectant murmur died with the houselights.
A few desultory chants of "Noades out" broke the nervous silence.
What was this in aid of ? Were we going to be merged, taken over, sold off ?
Sharing our ground was a big enough injury - was insult to be added ?
What devious plans did our dodgy Chairman have in mind ?
All was to be revealed. But first the preliminaries.
A funny man opened the proceedings with some good South London humour.
Then the potted history of the club (with slides) kept us amused.
The Directors, players and ground staff were introduced onto the stage to differing degrees of applause and indifference from the audience.
The cold silence of Big Ron's entrance was contrasted by Coppell's ovation.
Under the bright stage lights Noades looked shiftier than ever. Would you buy a second hand football team off this man? No ? But he'd sell it to you anyway.
And so he started selling us the Lifeline Scheme. We listened, openly sceptical.
His smooth line in patter sounded very convincing. Similar schemes had proved successful at other clubs.
And then it struck us. He wanted our money. The bastard was after our cash. No way !
But whats this ? Steve Coppell's telling us to support the scheme. Give him the money and he'd promise to buy new players. Not to mention the cash prizes, cars and holidays on offer.
My iron resolve dissolved like the Palace defence on a bad Saturday and I filled in the glossy leaflet.
For only £2 a week I was investing in the future of my club. For only £8 a month I was giving Steve the chance to strengthen our squad. For a mere £100 a year I was gonna get us back in the First Division ! Yeah ! Let's go ! Sign that form. Hand it in.
Dive down to the bar for free wine care of Lada cars and Intasun.
Grab that free grub. Watch that free video of Palace beating Man Utd 5-0.
Going up. Going up. Going up uP UP. Glory days were coming to Palace again.
Outside, in the real world, empty chip wrappers blew past the Fairfield Halls.

John Pateman

FANS

Cover Story

AN IMPERFECT MATCH
50p
LATE IN 88
BLOWING UP A STORM!
No.4
A LITTLE BLOWY AT HIGHBURY THESE DAYS, NIGEL.
THE WIND OF CHANGE, MA'AM.
I LIKE BEING AT THE CLOCK END
JVC
RIBALD,

NO 7

THE LION ROARs

THE ALTERNATIVE MILLWALL SUPPORTER'S MAGAZINE

50p

TV OR NOT TV?

WHO CARES

ITS TAKEN YOU LONG ENOUGH TO FIND THE DEN

BONUSPRINT

MILLWALL 2
Cascarino 1
Carter 42

NORWICH 2
Butterworth 2
Bowen 7

READ

THINGS THAT MAKE AN AWAY DAY MEMORABLE

1. THE ONE TURNSTILE AT OXFORD ..
2. THE PLASTIC PIE AT MAN UTD..
3. THE PISS CASCADE IN THE KOP EVERY DERBY DAY..
4. COCKNEY HOSPITALITY..
5. SUNDERLAND SINGING "EVERTON,EVERTON,WHERE'S YOUR SCARVES?"...
6. FLARES AND CENTREPARTS AT DERBY..
7. AMBERLINE COACHES NOT BREAKING DOWN..
8. THE PLAYER'S CLAPPING US BEFORE THEY GO OFF..
9. PAYING THE SAME TO GET IN AS HOME SUPPORTERS..

        What about the away end's at Coventry,Norwich,Man.City etc. etc.

When Skies Are Grey

IDenTity

Fortune's
ALWAYS HIDING
I.D. CARD

Beat the rush with your *Fortune's Always Hiding* ID CARD

Mr Moynihan's Card is due to come in to effect in two season's time but, as you are all aware, fails to deal with that thorny problem — trouble *off* the ground. As a public service *FAH* proudly presents, totally free with this issue, a card which takes care of violence wherever it may be!

Affix
Photo
Here

Fortune's
ALWAYS HIDING
IDENTITY CARD

The bearer of this card promises to be very, very good on and off the ground.

signature

FAH cannot accept responsibility for card holders who are naughty or well out of order.

NORTH BANK NORMAN SEZ...

"I WOULDN'T BE SEEN DEAD WITHOUT ONE."

The Soup

Dawn raid: Harriers fans held

Police today arrested 25 football fans in a dawn swoop they hope will smash the notorious Severn Valley Railway Firm.

Those held — all of them Kidderminster Harriers supporters — are alleged to have BUMPED into people when the lights have been off in the bogs at half-time

SPILT soup on the terraces by accident

SHOUTED a rude word at the referee when he made a bad decision

STEPPED on somebody's foot when trying to avoid the dog turds in the alley by the cattle market which never has any streetlights working.

The Severn Valley Railway Firm are notorious because of the highly organised nature of their spectating.

They infiltrate the terraces disguised as normal Harriers fans wearing anoraks, trousers and caps having first got up, had a good breakfast, gone shoppping, gone the pub, met the lads, had a few beers and walked to the ground.

But once the game is underway, they are alleged to have huddled together for warmth and annoyed three non-smokers nearby. On at least one occasion, three of the gang members stood in somebody else's place, it is claimed.

Some of the fans are expected to be charged under the new How Dare They Be At The Football When They Should Be Out Looking For A Job Act, recently introduced by the Government.

ROYALS GET WEMBLEY SHOCK!

"THEY ASKED TO SEE OUR MEMBERSHIP CARDS!"

"WHAT - THE WIFE TOO?"

n Shocks,
es, Worthing

CARDS ON THE TABLE TIME

Moynihan: Football Fan

Yes its the obligatory fanzine rant against the peril that is I.D. cards. You've probably seen and heard all these arguments a thousand times before, but we think that they can't be over-stressed until the scheme is thrown out. Surveys have shown that a huge majority of football supporters disagree with Moynihan's proposals, but unfortunately, like the coming poll-tax, dissent will not be widespread or fierce enough until the effects are actually felt.

The job of opposing the scheme has been made more difficult by the fact that Moynihan has not published it in detail. He has decided (or should we say she has decided) that something must be done, but he can't put the scheme into a legislative framework, because the technology isn't ready yet. An Enabling Bill has therefore been passed, a procedure frowned upon by most parliamentarians, which sets up a Football Membership Authority. The F.M.A. (which Jack Dunnett has intimated the league will join), is entrusted with the onerous task of setting up the scheme and ensuring it works. Moynihan can tinker with the scheme without reference to Parliament, which is (rather surprisingly for a Tory cabinet minister) completely anti-democratic.

One of the most annoying aspects of the membership debate has been the references to the situation at Luton. It has been constantly stressed how few arrests there are now, and the low the levels of policing. As long as the scheme is not going to ban away fans, (and God forbid we should ever be banned from watching Spurs away), these points are irrelevant to the present debate. Quite apart from the drop in average gates at Kenilworth Road during their most successful season ever, if anyone could actually be bothered to go to Luton and cause trouble, their scheme, which plainly doesn't work 100% would be severely dangerous. Ten years ago say, when violence did occur inside grounds, the Luton scheme, with its absence of proper stewarding, could have had disastrous effects.

One of the best arguments against the scheme is that it is not inside the ground where violence now occurs. Quite frankly, having followed Spurs everywhere this season it isn't outside the ground either but that's another story. Moynihan has at-tempted to produce tables of arrests around grounds to show that violence is still prevalent. Anyone who goes to games regularly knows that this is wrong. Violence inside grounds is almost non-existent today for two basic reasons. Firstly police tactics have improved greatly on matters such as segregation, cameras and keeping rival fans apart after the game (though West Ham showed how much they still have to learn). Witness the excellent job by the Middlesboro police who escorted us straight onto a free bus from the station to the ground and then cordoned off the whole road at our end. In many ways this is quite sad, but if it stops trouble which it plainly does, and we get a free bus ride, so be it. The second factor which has aided the first is the declining levels of aggression to be found in youth culture (all of it having passed to Wimbledon's No.4). Ten years ago youth culture was far more violent, with the gang mentality contributing to such problems as the rise of the National Front around grounds, which made them place of intense hatred rather than the (fairl of good natured rivalry which should and hop

---

Just Another Wednesday

The Spur

CRISIS

> Can I see your Membership Card, sir ?

The Macho Factor

1988 was the year in which "being in the club" was viewed as a good thing by our traditionalist government. The proposed introduction of an Identity Card Scheme is, of course, a gross infringement of civil liberty but well in keeping with the spirit of '88....the year in which the number of immigration officials was doubled; the G.C.H.Q. fight for the right to have a union continued; the chancellor outlined plans to means-test pensioners benefits; and the year in which democratically elected parties, whatever you think of them, were denied the right to be heard. The introduction of identity cards must be seen in its political context.

IDENTITY CRISIS
(THE ADVENT OF THE CARD SCHEME)

Many suspect that football is being used as a testing ground; more precisely that the introduction of compulsory I.D. is a step towards a national identity system along French lines whereby non-production of your card when demanded by an officer of the law can result in your arrest and continued detention until the "necessary" proof is furnished. The card scheme has little hope of success as it, in line with all Conservative politics, seeks to suppress the discontent born of its policies. The problem with Tory politics is that instead of implementing radical change in areas of severe depression, improving housing and creating real job prospects for example, they attack the needy, and when the needy turn round and bite the hand that doesn't provide, that hand cracks down,...but still refuses to address the rest of the problem; social decay.

What I'm not saying is that "Football Hooligans" are all homeless and living on the dole. This is only a part truth. Which leads me to another aspect of discussion - the role of machoism and the glorification of the male and male pride in football violence. Conservative politics, with its emphasis on possession - car, house, wife etc is directly linked to male violence. To be a "real" man, the male must have affluence and therefore power. Witness the rise of the Yuppie or the self-made millionaire held aloft as an ideal image; well-dressed, married, refined accent. If a man does not have these qualities, he must turn to that 'essential' characteristic; strength. Strength combined with deprivation means violence. This becomes the poor man's only viable means of protecting his maleness. It is at football grounds that this problem may be seen, bound up in clannishness, uniforms, notions of territories, class and racial divides. Is it any coincidence that the profile of racist groups reaches a high at periods of economic depression and makes itself visible particularly at soccer games... The football then becomes a breeding ground for frustrated maleness.

The problem, then, is enormous, and the solution is a deconstruction of this dangerous notion of the male. Only when this is achieved will violence be eased in the ground, outside the ground, in the home and on the streets. If anything the Introduction of Cards scheme is likely to increase levels of violence, in that it does not address the real problems of football violence in the context of rape, muggings, sex abuse and murder. Violence will merely be diverted at the turnstiles.

fully does occur today. Perhaps the F.S.A. has helped in this and should be congratulated (and joined immediately).

So the Bill is a total waste of time. But that's not all. It could also be a dangerous, total waste of time. This season's night games between Arsenal V Liverpool and Man. U.V Q.P.R., where around 20,000 people weren't in the ground at kick off time, would hardly have been helped by a membership scheme. Neither would the fiascos at West Ham and Arsenal that Spurs fans had to endure. Perhaps Moynihan is trying to help us with his scheme by driving fans away from the national game to prevent such overcrowding.

Anyway you must know all of this already so things to do now. Write to your M.P. at the House of Commons telling them what a complete waste of time the Bill is. Tell them if they don't do everything in their power to stop the Bill you will,

a) Stop voting for them and will instruct all family and friends to do the same.

b) Send Gazza round to eat them.

c) Make it compulsory for all M.P.s to sport Chrissy Waddle haircuts (I can just see Thatch now).

This should sort the problem out.

Matt Stone

TORYISM

> HELP US! HELP US! WE'RE STARVING

> WE'RE SO POOR!

> WE'RE SO COLD

BRADFORD 1988

City Gent

Cartoons and writing by Wendy Michallat

Andy Gray illustrates how much pace he's lost since he last played in Scotland

DANGER IN NUMBERS

The debacle at the Q.P.R. v West Ham cup-tie earlier this season should have come as no surprise to anyone who has seen at first hand the way that membership schemes have been introduced. Although these incidents took place some time ago, they have still not been satisfactorily explained, and important issues have not been settled. Paul Caulfield was our ace newshound on the spot...

When West Ham visited Q.P.R. in the F.A. Cup this season, we finally saw how chaotic and dangerous membership schemes could be. The match was supposedly all-ticket, though as we queued anxiously, inching our way towards the turnstiles, everyone was wondering if something had gone wrong. Our suspicions were confirmed when, once inside, we saw the dangerous overcrowding of the away end, contrasting with the empty spaces in the Q.P.R. seats.

The match started on time, but within three minutes, many people had scaled the barriers to escape the crush, and the teams were led off as the crowd encroached. For the next hour, confusion reigned as the stewards struggled to cope with the situation. Eventually, the extra West Ham supporters were found places in the main stand and the Rangers end.

The enforced pitch invasion drew a swift response from the mounted police, whose helmeted officers rode onto the pitch before lining up, paramilitary-style in the centre circle. This show of force was ridiculous and totally unnecessary, and was undoubtedly aimed at impressing the watching German police. These methods were later described in the *Today* newspaper as *"Softly, Softly"*.

Comedy

One of the horses provided the best entertainment of the day, in fact, as it strode purposefully towards the West Ham terrace and left a pile of steaming dung on the six-yard line. It would have been hard to find a more appropriate comment on events, and understandable cries of "shitty ground" went up from the compressed masses behind the goal. As it turned out, this effort was to prove more significant than anything West Ham did in either penalty area all afternoon.

After five more minutes of inactivity, we were treated to the sight of someone clearing the unwanted compost with a dustpan and brush. He attracted the pick of Fleet Street's photo-corps (*WSC* included, naturally) and the collective mirth of 25,000. Meanwhile, amid the hilarity, people hurt in the crush were stretchered from the terraces, as we heard, with disbelief, radio reports of 'crowd trouble' at Loftus Road. The game restarted just before four o'clock, and our patience was 'rewarded' with a West Ham performance of gutless ineptitude, resulting in a deserved 3-1 defeat. I was disappointed with the result, but

relieved at the peaceful outcome, and impressed with the way our supposed 'hooligans' had behaved. As we left, the official attendance was given at around 23,800. Q.P.R. apologised for the overcrowding, which they blamed on forged tickets, and thanked us for our co-operation.

The inquests began the following Monday. Hammersmith's Chief Superintendent, Michael Briggs, blamed the membership scheme for the problems: *"Membership schemes may work at some grounds, but I feel it is a nonsense. It is a problem we do not need. One end of the ground was half-full, and the other end was packed to capacity."* He made it clear to us that he was not against membership schemes *per se*, but that he felt that London's itinerant football support posed problems which could not be accommodated by the rigid scheme introduced by Rangers.

Q.P.R. secretary Ron Phillips also admitted that the membership scheme caused problems, and in addition re-iterated his view that there were approximately 600 forged tickets. Superintendent Briggs' estimate of the numbers in the Q.P.R. end was generous — in fact there were only 1,949 places taken up on the terrace out of a capacity of 4,500. Phillips agreed that the situation which arose had made a complete mess of the segregation at the match, and Q.P.R. are now considering changes which might be introduced. Already this season, following incidents at their match

with Chelsea in September, they had taken the East side of the South Africa Road paddock out of the scheme.

Drama

However, according to what Phillips has to say, Superintendent Briggs is being unduly modest in blaming everything on the membership scheme and the forged tickets, since his own force were by no means content with a walk-on role in the drama. As visitors to other London grounds (e.g. Spurs and Chelsea) will have noticed this season, the police have been experimenting with metal detectors as an additional means of checking away fans for anything they shouldn't be carrying (such as money, keys etc). The West Ham match was the first in which these machines (borrowed from Gatwick Airport) had been in action at Loftus Road.

Since they went off virtually every time someone went through, this inevitably slowed the passage of fans on to the terrace almost to a trickle. As a result, there were apparently almost 2,000 people still outside the ground at kick-off time. Hearing the whistle for the start of the game, these fans (according to Mr Phillips) rushed the turnstiles, breaking some of them down and climbing over others. This, apart from the forged tickets, was the main reason for the overcrowding, as (again, in Mr Phillips' opinion) many of these fans were without tickets.

This explanation is not totally satisfactory, although if true, it would indicate almost unbelievable stupidity on the part of the police in insisting on the worthless metal detectors. Superintendent Briggs denied that the detectors had caused the problem. What about the 'rushing' of the turnstiles? Anyone who has stood cursing outside a ground unable to get in as kick-off time approaches, will know how difficult it is for a crowd to surge through turnstiles by sheer force of numbers, especially if there is a substantial police presence, including horses, as there was in this case. Again, the police cast doubt on Phillips' version of events — they claim that *one* turnstile jammed half-open, and that this was the only place where people could have climbed over. Another question also presents itself. Why would fans without tickets bother queuing outside entrances which specifically stated that tickets were necessary to get in?

There are two plausible alternatives to Phillips' theory. Firstly, that too many people were admitted to the terrace because the turnstile operators were accepting cash instead of tickets. This was suggested in a letter to *When Saturday Comes* published in the la...

Not a lot of people know that little spotty Colin Moynihan was one of the pitch invaders who went into hysterics, waving, tip-o'-tailing and generally having a super time when the Great Britain hockey team won the gold in Seoul.

FILTH AND SCUM

Had he done this "celebrating" at a soccer match abroad he would have been baton charged, shown over and over again on the news, labelled "filth and scum" by the tabloids and then had some Government toe-rag clerk forcing a compulsory members bill down his throat.

issue. Phillips accepts that some of the 700 previously unsold tickets were exchanged for cash on the day (in contravention of F.A. rules), but insists that this was on the direct instructions of the police, and that it only occurred just before the kick-off, in order to ease the pressure outside the turnstiles (which was caused by the police in the first place, according to him!). However, our correspondent, Simon Lord, got into the ground at around 1.30 pm, and reported seeing cash on the counter at that time.

Secondly, it is surely not impossible that the police simply decided to let everyone in, whether with tickets, money or neither, to prevent serious disturbances outside the ground. Supt. Briggs states without reservation that police would at no time stop searching people entering the ground, no matter how slow this would make the process.

What is indisputable is that both the club and the police lay some of the blame on the membership scheme, citing the half-empty home end as evidence. Phillips' reasoning is this — the Q.P.R. fans who were not members had to be accommodated in the East End of the South Africa Road paddock, which, in other circumstances, would have been given over to West Ham fans. Thus, West Ham had a smaller area in which to fit the same number of fans, and the crush developed as a result. This would be a reasonable proposition if the game hadn't been all-ticket, but of course it was. Assuming that Q.P.R. didn't sell too many tickets for the West Ham end, either in advance or on the day, the possible reasons for the extra numbers are limited to four:

1) They got in on forged tickets
2) They rushed the turnstiles without tickets
3) They were allowed in by the police just after kick-off, without tickets.
4) Q.P.R. accepted cash on the turnstiles.

Probably we will never know the real answer, but any of the four lays the club and/or the police open to serious charges of incompetence, or worse. If the tickets were forgeries, the turnstile counters should have told that the terrace was overcrowded before it was too late. If the crowd rushed the turnstile (and of course they shouldn't have been still outside the ground anyway), the police must have been incredibly lax. If the police let them in regardless, they can only take the entire blame for what happened. If Q.P.R. accepted cash, they are in a very serious position indeed, and such an irresponsible action could have been responsible for a major tragedy.

Farce

The club's only defence lies in the assertion that the turnstiles were rushed, since this was the only thing that could reasonably have prevented them counting and controlling the number of people entering the terrace. If this *was* the case, then the membership scheme is irrelevant, since, in his version, the build-up outside the turnstiles was caused by completely different factors (i.e. the metal detectors). Since Ron Phillips continues to insist that the membership scheme *was* to blame, *and* has now told us that he doesn't think the forgeries were a very significant factor after all, this throws considerable doubt on the turnstile-rushing theory. It borders on the farcical to suggest that one half-open turnstile, with police in attendance, was responsible for admitting 2,000 or so ticketless fans, who had been hopefully queuing outside a ticket-only entrance.

The evidence points more and more to the possibility that the turnstile operators had been accepting cash well before kick-off time.

Reactions elsewhere have not focused on these questions. The F.A. were characteristically tight-lipped (if not ashen-faced) about the whole thing. They said they had a report from their representative at the match, but that it was confidential, and suggested we contact the League for more information. To his credit, the F.A. spokesman stressed that there was no 'trouble' at the game, though the press had other ideas, as the **'Crowd Trouble'** headlines proved.

The League were much more helpful. Press officer Andy Williamson confirmed that they had always had doubts about membership schemes, and were never sold on the idea that they could combat hooliganism:

"We plan to re-examine the arrangement at the end of the season, and more information will be available for the clubs soon. We are also concerned with the delay in dealing with the situation at Q.P.R. and feel that this was due to the membership scheme". He gave special praise to the supporters: *"The crowd behaved impeccably considering the delay, and everyone involved should be complimented. It showed that most football supporters are patient people, and that the vast majority behave responsibly".* This statement does not seem to tie in particularly well with Ron Phillips' graphic images of impatient and irresponsible West Ham fans breaking through the turnstiles.

Many people have had doubts about membership schemes, ever since they were forced on the clubs at the start of the season. The Football Supporters Association recently produced a report entitled *Membership or Registration?*, which was highly critical of the schemes at many league clubs. The report found that membership schemes usually failed to deter hooliganism, often made crowd control more difficult, and caused inconvenience to, and restriction of, supporters. The report condemned Q.P.R.'s scheme as *"comfortably (or uncomfortably) the worst in the whole country"*. As we have now seen, its findings were borne out to the letter.

Some clubs have relaxed their schemes, or never fully implemented them on police advice, and the League will no doubt press the Sports Minister to allow further relaxations next season. But with the Government's reputation for (not) listening, the protestations of the League are likely to fall on deaf ears. This promises little for supporters, who are still likely to face the same problems, or worse,

next season. The only advice now on offer is to buy a season-ticket, or to get to the matches an hour before everybody else. Perhaps the most frightening conclusion to emerge from this sorry affair, and the one which should concern supporters the most, is that **NO-ONE REALLY KNOWS WHAT HAPPENED**. The theories of Q.P.R. and the police, supposedly acting in harmony to combat hooliganism and facilitate crowd control are totally at odds with one another — this, if nothing else, indicates a complete abdication of responsibility.

Tragedy

Meanwhile, the government, Q.P.R., and other clubs who have seen fit to introduce their schemes in equally short-sighted ways, might like to reflect on some words from the enquiry into the Burnden Park disaster in 1946, when 33 people died:

"How easy it is for a dangerous situation to arise in a crowded enclosure. It happens again and again without fatal, or even injurious consequences. But its danger is that it requires so little influence — an involuntary sway, an exciting moment, a comparatively small addition to the crowd, the failure of one part of one barrier — to translate the danger in terms of death and injuries".

Or again, on this description of the Ibrox disaster in 1971:

"They died in the most horrible circumstances. Some died underneath a pile of bodies ten feet high, all laid the same way, a wall of heads and faces, most with their tongues lolling out. Some died on their feet, squeezed out of their shoes by the crush of bodies, shoes which were later found on the stairway slimy with urine and vomit."

No-one was killed, or even seriously injured at Loftus Road, although they almost certainly would have been if there had been fences in front of the terrace. Ironically, there is a sign at West Ham's own ground, warning people to leave slowly, which says: **'Remember Ibrox'**. Do they? Or Bradford? Or Heysel? Are we really still waiting for yet more disasters? Or, even worse, creating the very conditions in which they are likely to occur? The report by the F.A. into the events at Q.P.R. is not going to be made public. When are we going to get some answers?

Paul Caulfield & Mike Ticher

IDenTiTy CRisiS

Charlton Athletic supporters have had much to put up with over the last few years, bankruptcy and groundsharing being the most obvious traumas.

But as if we hadn't suffered enough we now find the Sports Minister, resplendent in his now famous Charlton tie, continually boasting about his support for the club.

If Mr Moynihan really supported Charlton, or had the slightest understanding of what the club is about, then he would hardly be promoting the present 100% membership proposals.

For if the scheme is irrelevant to football's hooligan problem as a whole, then nowhere is it more irrelevant than at Charlton. In the words of the QPR secretary:

"When we play Charlton all my matchday staff relax completely because they are aware that they are dealing with some of the most civilised and well-behaved fans in the Football League."

Charlton are one of sixteen clubs who have said that if the scheme is implemented they could be forced out of business. Yet thus far the club's response to the scheme has been equivocal.

As Charlton supporters we disown Mr Moynihan and resent his attempt to latch onto our club for his own political purposes. Instead of publicising his views within the matchday programme, we would like to see Charlton disown him too.

And the next time Mr Moynihan feels inclined to visit the directors box at a Charlton home match, we urge Mr Norris to show him a card of his own.

A red one.

HARRIERS IN HOOLIGANISM SENSATION

NEW figures compiled 15 years ago but released today by Sports Minister Colin Moynihan reveal that GM Vauxhall Conference side Kidderminster Harriers have the worst hooliganism problem in the world.

Harriers come top of a "league table of shame" of football-related arrests compiled by the uniformed wing of the Conservative Party, the Association of Chief Police Officers.

The statistics show that Kidderminster police arrested over 900,000 hooligans for football-related offences last season — more than 20 times the club's total attendance.

None of those arrested, however, were charged.

Harriers have defended their record, pointing out that only three of the 900,000 arrests took place inside the ground, and they were Cabinet ministers caught soliciting for immoral purposes round the back of the toilets.

The other "football-related offences" included:
● A woman caught shoplifting in Sainsbury's who had a Harriers sticker in her car.
● A fan caught breaking into his own car who had a match programme in his pocket.
● A Colombian cocaine farmer who was given a lapel badge by a missionary.
● The blind tailor who sells small-but-perfectly-formed Jon Pearson his suits.

Mr Mywhatabrowntongueivegotyhan said: "These shocking statistics just go to prove what I have been saying all along.

"Decent, law-abiding people and families have been staying away from matches in droves because of the constant threat of widespread violence and rioting...and because they don't like football. (Don't quote that).

"Under my plans for compulsory ID cards, a football match will be a place to take the family for the day with large open spaces of terracing where children can play safely without the constant risk of another Heysel tragedy."

Referring to allegations that he doesn't know his arse from his elbow as far as football is concerned, Mr Lapdog countered: "That is an outrageous slur.

"I have been a regular football supporter since I was knee-high to a salmonella virus. I've been to every single FA Cup final for the past three years. And the European Cup final. And the World Cup final. And the hockey at the Olympics."

Meanwhile, a protest petition signed by every single person in the world was yesterday handed in at 10 Downing Street. Mr Moynihan said: "I know best".

the LAD's DAD's guide to

87 Of course it never used to happen in my day!They should be tied to the goalposts and birched. It would bring the crowds back as well!Brian Clough had the right idea. *

88 I think this plan is the only answer, if you've got to carry a photo with you,you're not going to get in trouble.It will be good to come to a game without fear of violence.

89 You're wasting your time with this petition lark, son.It's as good as Law already and most law-abiding fans think it's a good thing.

90 So here we are, the first day of the new scheme. No sign of any trouble, a return of families to soccer grounds.Ah! It's just like the Golden Age of football again.

Yes the Big match!What a delight to see queues of people flocking back to the game. And all because of a little card. "Er, Dad you haven't got an identity card."

Don't worry about me!! no troublemaker... "But Dad..." I'll get in old Joe the turnstile knows "Yes...but you need card."

91 It's alright officer, I'm in the Conservative Club Here's my affiliation card.I think you'll find it's all in order.

"GOOD AFTERNOON TO BOTH SETS OF SUPPORTERS, THE SMITHS AND THE BROWNS. TODAY'S OPPONENTS SHOULD BE ROTHERHAM, IF THEY CAN RAISE THE BUS FARE.

92 It's just as I said this scheme will stop the hooligan it drives real fa

* PLEASE NOTE: THIS IS AN ANACHRONISM

The Soup

Lookalike

waste of space

Fenwick

The Spur

Sirs
I wonder whether any of your readers have noticed the striking resemblance between Terry Fenwick and a waste of space. Are they by any chance related?
Dom Jessop
Walthamstow
London

Having some more cake and eating it...

"Unfortunately, we have had consistent complaints and criticism from the Police regarding the `Shelf area', where far too many arrests occur at most matches"
Irving Scholar
letter to member of LOTS
12th April 1988

"As far as my own club is concerned, last season more than 600,000 attended home matches and 73 people were arrested inside and outside the ground. This figure (which includes touts selling tickets at enhanced values) taken as a percentage is 0.01 meaning 99.99 per cent were law-abiding..."
Irving Scholar
speech to House of Lords
24th January 1989

LINCOLN HOOLIES

The Banker Magazine

There has been a big response to the article in issue one entitled "HOOLIES...WHO?"

THE BANKER must again stress that we reject the notion of a "Football" hooligan. Hooliganism (whatever the word means) is the problem of society and is not the fault of football (take away football and they'd go somewhere else.)

At Lincoln there has not been any serious trouble for a long time. I remember 5-10 years ago when there was the odd flare-up when we played teams like Sheffield Wednesday, Derby, Doncaster, and Scunthorpe. But on the whole there has never been much of a problem at Lincoln.

However, a couple of years ago a new group emerged calling itself L.T.E. (Lincoln Transit Elite.) Although small in number, it attracted a great degree of police attention as I discovered when travelling down to Kettering on the Inter City train last season.

I recount a conversation I overheard while standing in the carriage...

Youth... "why are there so many police on this train?"
Officer... "because we have to watch you."

Youth..."Who are we?"
Officer... "You're the famous L.T.E."

The youth and the police officer then had a very friendly little chat about who had been arrested that day, where the police had boarded the train, police tactics, etc, etc. Any observer would have thought they were best mates!

Of course, L.T.E. gained national fame after the New Year's Eve riot two years ago, and as usual the scandal press distorted the issue to blame football. The fact that a few people were chanting "L.T.E." during the riot was reported by the press as "SOCCER RIOT IN LINCOLN"!

'CUP of WOE'

26 arrests will hit the anti-card campaign

MANCHESTER — City fans, arrested at their club's Cup tie in London delivered a blow to the anti-ID card campaign.

Police detained 26 Blues fans when fighting broke out on the terraces, during the match with Brentford.

Scotland Yard said today that most of the arrests at Griffin Park were for drunken or threatening behaviour. A number of police officers received minor injuries in the clashes.

Although police praised the "exemplary behaviour" of the majority of City fans, they said they are "disappointed" at the number of arrests.

Most of those detained were later sent home to Manchester, but some may appear in courts later.

Violence inside the ground will add weight to the government's plans to bring in identity cards for fans.

Fans in battle as City go out

More trouble came as City in the 75th minute. With Jones receiving treatment following a clash with McNab and the game held up. Dibble inexplicably raced 30 yards from his goal to remonstrate with the referee and was immediately given the yellow card.

Two minutes later trouble erupted among the City fans and police reinforcements were hastily called in with several supporters dragged from the terraces.

The many unfortunate (or should I say fortunate!) City fans who missed out on the meagre ticket allocation for the FA Cup 4th round tie at Brentford were no doubt perplexed at the reports of terrace violence by Blues fans and subsequent arrests. Press comment that the trouble strengthened the Governments case for ID cards was in itself disturbing.

In fact, a truer version of events has to take account of incidents on the pitch which influenced crowd behaviour and must also include over-reaction on the part of the police.

But first to set the scene. It poured heavily before the kick off and the rain continued for most of the game. The City section consisted of an open end terrace plus the end of a covered terrace alongside the pitch. Due to the weather the majority of City fans were tightly packed under the meagre shelter to the extent that spaces on the adjacent open terrace made it look as though City had been short-changed on their ticket allocation (perhaps they had). The jostling for places under cover inevitably resulted in fans occasionally falling forward down the terracing, but as ever there was good humour from the 'inflatable brigade'.

Fifteen minutes from the final whistle one of Neil McNab's over-zealous tackles flattened Brentford's Jones almost on the touchline. Their trainer came on but despite the player being not too badly hurt treatment continued on the pitch rather than off it. The referees refusal to order the Brentford duo over the touchline, and thus letting play continue, understandably angered the City players who wanted to get on with the game and avoid time-wasting. To this end Andy Dibble ran out of his goal area to put this point to the ref. (The ever-so-in-touch Peter Gardener, in that evenings pink, referred to Dibble's

behaviour as 'inexplicable').

For his pains Andy received the yellow card, this act of discipline taking place right in front of the packed section of Blues on the covered terrace. The reaction of the crowd was to be expected: shouting, gesticulating and in general letting off steam in the usual manner which has occurred for over a century throughout the football world in response to such incidents. Matters would have returned to 'normal' in a couple of minutes once the game restarted but because of the numbers on the small area of terracing the crowd surged forward at one point. There were already some police amongst the fans, but within seconds a large force went en masse over the touchline wall, with truncheons drawn. The police were pulling out people left right and centre, some carrying horrendously dangerous weapons (Bananas). Predictably the random ejections and arrests sparked off even more disturbance, pushing and shoving, falling, people trying to get out of the way. Some semblance of order eventually returned, but at the cost of an unsavoury atmosphere of bitter resentment and further alienation between police and the ordinary supporter.

There was no justification for over-reaction by the police, but sadly such heavy handed behaviour has become prevalent at many games in the recent post Luton and post Heysel seasons. In a climate of impending ID card legislation, tainted with the notorious police infiltration operations, (Omega et al) the police force knows it has the upper hand and, with a confidence bordering on arrogance, acts and reacts accordingly.

But what protection is an ID card against a trunceon and why did my mate's daughter get a boot on her head at Brentford, merely for being in the way?

HOOLIGAN PAGE

The gentleman on the right of course is not a hooligan. He is a Rugby Union supporter who is just showing a bit of high spirits at the Leicester versus Barbarians game that took place last December.

Just Another Wednesday

About 200 Millwall supporters tried 'Operation Get Into Kenilworth Road' Only about 50 succeeded, with great foresight those people like myself applied early this season for membership. May I suggest many more out there do so early next season (If they stay up) and all congregate say in E Block Main Stand so our voices will be as one. Not that those of us who did get in last Saturday didn't do the club justice, I'm sure we 50 made more noise than the 7,000 crap that Luton put together. I know the club has good reason to be weary of us but they are becoming neurotic to the point of refusing the guests of their own fans admission.

When I rang their soccer line during the week before the game some wally on the recorded message proudly announced 'Most clubs are envious of Luton's membership scheme' What utter bullshit. All this has done for Luton is to isolate them from other clubs, to become their own empty little prison void of any atmosphere, situated in a shit heap of a town.

The feeling in the ground was lacking and stale, you could sense we were not welcome even though no colours were being worn by us and against all good intentions of not jumping up and shouting if we scored I'm afraid emotions got the better of me when Tony crossed for Carter's first goal which was magic.

The Lion Roars

SPOT THE MINISTER!

CHARLTON ATHLETIC FOOTBALL CLUB WELCOME YOU TO SELHURST PARK

Play SPOT THE MINISTER! The exciting new game for all the family.

Using your skill and judgement simply mark an X on the picture nearest where you think the Sports Minister is standing.

The person whose cross, in the opinion of the judges, is nearest the Sports Minister in the crowd will be named the winner and they will receive an autographed membership card.

The editors accept as a matter of faith that the Sports Minister is in the crowd and point out that they can accept no responsibility for tall people who might stand in front of him

Sponsored by GEC, a company likely to make a large amount of money out of developing something completely pointless.

Useful information

1. There was not an election pending when the picture was taken.

2. Punching the air can be a criminal offence at football matches.

3. Punching the air is not a criminal offence at hockey matches.

4 Colin Moynihan used to claim Charlton were in his constituency.

5. Colin Moynihan is MP for Lewisham East.

6. There are many Charlton and Millwall supporters living in Lewisham East.

7. Mr Moynihan does not have a big majority.

8. There will be a General Election in 1991.

IDenTity CRisis

BE OUR PEST

There is one hope that all of us here today have in common. That my tenure as Minister for Sport will not end in the same way as that of my predecessors - with the sack. At the moment there is no means of ensuring that that will be avoided.

Month in, month out since 1979 Mrs Thatcher has been sacking ministers. The last parliament's number of dismissals and demotions was an all-time record. Only the other week we had the enforced departure of Mrs Edwina Currie for threatening behaviour.

That is why I fully agree with the Daily Express and the Daily Mail when they publish the editorials we at Central Office send them.

"Steadily and surely the Government is moving to crack down on the non-productive and old-fashioned, working-class activities that Mrs Thatcher does not understand. Let there be no slackening."

The membership scheme will be a major step forward in my political career. For the first time it will be possible to force uneconomic and decaying football clubs to the wall. As things

Colin Moanalot is Minister for Sport.

He has been a Charlton supporter ever since it was pointed out to him that he is the right height to join the board of directors.

stand there is nothing to stop generous benefactors luring supporters back to the terraces long after the clubs should have been destroyed by insolvency. Now we will be able to identify newcomers and make it impossible for them to gain admission.

For the companies developing the system I am determined that it should be as profitable as possible. Modern technology means that we can justify all kinds of sophisticated hardware which will really serve no useful purpose at all. And any supporters who do manage to acquire cards will feel the full weight of a mountain of junk mail, the most effective punishment available.

But the scheme need not destroy efficiently run clubs. There are more EXECUTIVE BOXES today at Luton than there were EXECUTIVE BOXES before their 100% membership scheme began. And there has been not one nuclear holocaust at Luton since the scheme was introduced.

As a politician I am completely indifferent to the effect this will have on Charlton. I well remember the good old days and being passed down over the heads of the crowd in order that I might gain a better view of such heroes as Jim Melrose and Mark Stuart.

At least in the future I will have the terraces and stands entirely to myself.

COLIN MOANALOT
Minister for Sport

Voice of the Valley

GREAT MOMENTS IN CHELSEA HISTORY (2)

'THE CAT' TWISTS THROUGH THE AIR TO PULL OFF ANOTHER FANTASTIC SAVE

Chelsea Independent

FACE IN THE CROWD

BOLTON EVENING NEWS

If you can prove that the person circled is you then you have won yourself free beer (vimto for the under 18's) for the rest of your life.

Normid Nomad

AMUSING NOT ABUSING

PRETENTIOUS OR WHAT?

FROM BEHIND YOUR FENCES
The Independent Boston United
football fanzine

30p
issue
3

NOT ON SALE TO ANYONE
WITHOUT A SENSE OF HUMOUR

YOU DIRTY NORTHERN SCUM

WE REFUSE TO OPENLY GENUFLECT TO REALMS OF SOCIAL STEREO-TYPING

YOU USE SPLIT INFINITIVES, WE DON'T, WE DON'T....AAARRRGH

CITY

CITY

BOST
SACK TH
BOAR

UNITED
JOHN 3.16

IF THIS PERSISTS, I MAY HAVE TO HURT SOMEONE

Nutcase Supporters From Around The World: In 1919 Charlton Athletic had a fishmonger fan who frequently attended matches carrying, not a banner, not even a scarf, not a stick.Well, I Charlton/Rangers bobble hat, but, of all things, a haddock nailed to a suppose he couldn't find a red herring.

Storming With Menace

VITAL: "FBYF" IS BANNED BY THE CLUB SO REMEMBER TO SWALLOW YOUR COPY AFTER READING

They Embarrassed The Hoops

No.8 Jim Conway

Not The View

James Payne rummages through the graveyard of Celtic's failed heroes to exhume another candidate for our Hall Of Infamy.

Thirty years on since he made his debut, Jim Conway is to most Celtic fans a forgotten figure. But at the time he played he was among the most discussed figures of the day. As Pat Woods and Tom Campbell hint in 'The Glory and The Dream', he was seen by many as a symbol of all that was frustrating about the most frustrating period in the Club's history.

What made Conway different from Byrne, Divers and others who played in the era and following the 7:1 game and which lasted seven years?

Well, unlike the others and despite many opportunities to prove himself, he always looked a terrible player. Possessor of the largest arse ever seen in the land until the emergence of the Duchess of York and a US Army regulation crewcut, he certainly did not look the part either. Although perhaps not as completely untalented as Maxwell, his goalscoring record of 13 goals in just over three seasons does give a hint that perhaps he was not the most gifted centre-forward in the Club's history.

Probably the most frustrating thing about Conway was the circumstances of his signing for Celtic in the first place.

The scout went to see two forwards who were playing for the junior side Coltness United. The player signed was Jim Conway. The player not signed was Joe Baker, who was twice the top scorer in Scotland, and is one of the very few players before the advent of the Dirty Dozen to have played for England whilst playing for a Scottish club (there's no truth in the rumour that the scout was John Kelman Snr).

And yet, despite his uselessness, Conway was not barracked by the supporters, who sensed that perhaps Jim realised he should not have been a Celtic player at all and that he was a real trier as well. Instead, come a Monday morning and Conway had failed to score yet again the previous Saturday, Celtic fans would respond to the taunts of their Hun colleagues with phrases like "A couple of years and he'll be a great player", "A couple of goals next week and he'll be scoring like McGrory" and "piss off, at least he's better than Don Kitchenbrand". Soon, three and a half years had passed and the same excuses were still being used.

In 'The Glory and The Dream', the phrase "The Jim Conway Syndrome" is used. To Celtic fans of the time, any syndrome associated with Jim would have had a different name!

But in reality it wasn't Jim Conway who embarrassed the hoops, it was the people who persisted in playing him long after he should have been confined to playing the piano.

Winifred Atwell was 87.

The Alex Smith signing criteria

... he's a lumberjack and he's OK!

The Northern Light

Storming With Menace

Bananas Bananas

Minister for Sport, Colin Moynihan, issues this statement to all football fans:

"From the beginning of the 1989/90 season there will be 100% compulsory membership of the Football League. Anyone who isn't carrying a banana or other inflatable will be refused entry to a football ground. The reason being to stop all violence at football matches and anyone causing trouble will have their banana, or other inflatable, taken away from them."

Fan: "What trouble?"

Minister for Sport: "See, it's working already."

THEY EMBARRASED THEMSELVES.   (No.2 in a series sampled from Not The View)

IAN CHRISTIE - The Man, The Myth, THE OWN GOAL

Ian Christie played only one match for Montrose, but that was one too many. The match in question took place on Saturday April 25th 1987, when promotion hopefuls Morton came to Links Park looking for the points to clinch promotion. With star goalkeeper Ray Charles having moved to sunny Methil for only £30,000, Montrose were left with a major problem-who to put in goal.

The previous week Grant Clark, on trial from Downfield had starred in goal, but he refused to sign. To this day nobody knows why. Along came Mr Ian Christie from Dundee Violet to help us out. What a joke - this keeper was crap! When he took the field you just had to laugh - about 4 feet tall (and that's being kind), balding and looking around 40. Was Ian Stewart serious? In the warm-up it was obvious he couldn't even dive to save the ball. Ian looked good to start with, but things started to go badly wrong. In the 39th minute Lex Richardson (now with our friendly neighbours Arbroath) put Morton into the lead by sliding the ball easily past Christie, who seemed to take an eternity to dive for the ball.

If the Montrose fans thought that was bad, even worse was to follow. A Morton player crossed the ball, and Christie dropped the ball when McNeil went to challenge him and Rowan Alexander poked the ball home - 2-0 Morton, and they were on their way back into the Premier League (albeit not for long.)

Mo Mo Super Mo

WHOOPS!

The third in our acclaimed series "They Refused to play for Wednesday" looks at a player that underwent a significant upheaval rather than go to Hillsborough:

Number three: Graeme Hogg.

During his only decent run in Manchester United's first team last season Hogg helped his team to rise from fifth to third, yet he has never really had the 'big club' profile that seems to be demanded by the Old Trafford hierarchy. Short of pace, he was never the ideal partner for Steve "Ugly great slow bastard" Bruce, the club's new, inexplicably expensive centre-half.

Enter Sheffield Wednesday. Although they had the improving Nigel Pearson the injury to Ian Knight had left them with only the ancient Lawrie Madden at centre-half. Madden played 38 times last season, far more than anyone of his age should have to, so a new centre-half was very much a priority for The Owls. With Kevin Moran and Paul McGrath getting over injury at Old Trafford Hogg became available but, when faced with an inquiry from the Sheffielders, Graeme refused to be panicked; in an action that spoke far more eloquently than a bookful of words he dropped down a division and moved about two hundred and fifty miles, to newly-relegated Portsmouth!

Flashing Blade

_____

The Crooked Spireite

The fourth in our incisive insight into those players who cried "Foul!" when approached by the Owls turns the spotlight from one area where Wednesday are crap (defending) to another area where Wednesday are crap, attacking. This month, we look at

Number 4: Dennis Wise.

Dennis, who along with Bristol City's "Stumpy" Galliers must rank as one of the shortest players ever to play for Dave Bassett, first shot to fame in an unfamiliar role at Wimbledon: as a skillful footballer, rather than some old clogger.

Having earned a reputation as an attacking player his greatest performance was, ironically, as a defender, doing a man-for-man marking job on John Barnes at Wembley that so stifled the creative Liverpool player that Howard Wilkinson came to take an interest in Wise, seeing himperhaps as a full-back to complement Mel Sterland rather than as a supplier of crosses for the likes of Lee Chapman. Basking in the euphoria of his club's Cup win Wise frequently repeated a desire to leave Plough Lane throughout the summer; mysteriously, he has dropped the subject since Wednesday declared their interest!

Soccer manager-speak – a guide to interpretation

I can't see myself ever leaving this club (I have no imagination whatsoever)

The Board is right behind me (I'm open to offers)

In this game you make your own luck (All our goals were offside)

Anything can happen in a cup tie (Please God, don't let us get beaten by a non-league side)

It's what happens over the 90 minutes that counts (We've been pathetic in training)

We're taking each game as it comes (I can't see beyond tomorrow)

I've got a lot of respect for Bobby Robson (They should give me his job)

Brian Moore's Head

Three minutes later Morton scored again. Christie unsurprisingly fumbled a shot and Alexander had an easy tap-in, with Christie still trying to differentiate his arse from his elbow! Gary Murray the super sub, made the scoreline more respectable when he scored a 'Charger' special after beating the Morton defence with his mazy run. The best goal of the whole match came just a minute later. Montrose's star midfielder Neil "I never score" Forbes attempted to pass back to midget Christie, who was standing at the edge of the box and the ball bounced over his head and into the net, for a quite majestic goal. The feat of Neil Forbes scoring a goal was a rare sight for Montrose fans, even though it was at the wrong end. It would take another 12 years for Mo fans to see this rare achievement once more (and that was a cracker as well.) Ian Christie's first senior appearance in Scottish football was also his last, and he buggered off back to Dundee Violet to play in the Junior league – thank God for that!!! There has been a rumour circulating that Ian Christie has changed his name by deed poll and is back in senior football as:-IAN ANDREWS. MMSM can exclusively reveal that this is a vicious lie, as there is one major difference between the two Ians- IAN ANDREWS IS ENGLISH.

John Wark he must be insane Either that or he hasn't a brain He once played for the blues And has decided to choose To play for them all over again.

The Citizen

RIVALS

The Lion Roars

WEST **h**AM DOWNGRADED
STUNNER

EAST LONDON WAS STUNNED TODAY WHEN ILEA ANNOUNCED THAT THEY WERE OFFICIALLY DOWNGRADING THE WEST HAM UNITED ACADEMY OF FOOTBALL TO A TECHNICAL COLLEGE....

'They've hardly warrented the title for years, they have had a few passes but no results and this year's inadequacies have brought matters to a head, they've misguided the press and TV commentators too long.' Said a spokesman for the Inner London Education Authority.

We tried to get a response from Hammers fans but the cheerful chirpy cockneys were far too busy dashing in and out of each others houses borrowing cups of sugar. We managed to contact ex-Irons supremo Pope Ron Greenwood II at his headquarters in the Vatican Arms and he told us. 'It's a great shame, but if you buy me another creme de menthe shandy I'll spill the beans'.

All attempts to reach current West Ham boss John Rockabilly Lyall failed as he dashed from the Trumpton Park ground pushing photographers aside yellin 'Leave me alone I've got a gig with Matchbox tonight..'

Pope Ron

John Lyall

SPOONER GLOBAL COMMUNICATIONS INC.

20 over-used facts about Millwall

1. Millwall are in the East End of London.

2. Every game at The Den is a right old Cockney knees-up.

3. Tony Cascarino was once transferred for a set of tracksuits and some corrigated iron. (Boring)

4. This is their first season in the First Divison after 103 years. (Even more boring).

5. Millwall always beat Charlton.

6. Millwall believe they are the biggest club in SE London.

7. This is not true.

8. We are.

9. Terry Hurlock is mean and fearsome.

10. Every time Millwall are mentioned in the papers, the words "Old Kent Road" are sure to follow.

11. Every one of the 20,000 fans who went to the Liverpool match has been a regular for forty years.

12. The Den is a well-appointed and spacious ground with a particularly inviting visitors' enclosure.

13. It is also extremely easy to find.

14. John Docherty is a dour Scotsman.

15. All Millwall fans eat jellied eels and say "Cor blimey, Guvnor!"

16. When they were televised live on two successive Sundays recently they were stuffed out of sight. (We are rather fond of this one.)

17. Harry Cripps and Barry Kitchener were "loyal servants" of the club.

18. Referees and visiting fans always get a good reception at The Den.

19. Millwall have a creche on matchdays.

20. They sing "no-one likes us", but it is not true any more. The South London Press thinks they are wonderful.

Steve Dixon

"COUNTRY ROADS TAKE ME HOME TO THE PLACE WHERE I BELONG."

The Hanging Sheep

Voice of the Valley

the bandwagon grows!

Here we see undeniable proof of the growing support for the sagheads. Pictured above are the merry troops on route to Trumpton for the 1:1 derby last month;a few well-wishers see the travel club off from Stapleton Road.And contrary to popular belief,as you can clearly see, they do have some fans over 12 years of age(and under 95).

The Bountyhunter

Under the Criminal Procedure (Scotland) Act, 1975
In the Sheriff Court of Glasgow and Strathkelvin at Glasgow

THE COMPLAINT OF THE PROCURATOR FISCAL against

ALISTAIR McCOIST;
RAYMOND WILKINS;
KEVIN DRINKELL and
MARK WALTERS
all c/o Rangers Football Club
lbrox Stadium
Edmiston Drive
GLASGOW

The charge against you is that

whilst acting with other members of Rangers Football Club,on 27 August 1988, during a training exercise then taking place at lbrox Football Stadium, Edmiston Drive, Glasgow, you did, with the intention of grossly embarassing supporters of Celtic Football Club and of inciting them to leave the said Stadium in droves before the conclusion of said training exercise, conduct yourselves in a disorderly manner and a) repeatedly strike the back of the Celtic net, on at least five occasions, with a football or similar unstoppable object; (b) repeatedly shaft Mick McCarthy, an employee of Celtic Football Club, then attempting to get a kick at said football; (c) make a cunt clown of Roy Aitken, then attempting to get a kick at you ALISTAIR McCOIST; (d) place said suporters of Celtic Football Club in such a state of utter dejection and ill-will towards the leiges that there-after they committed various acts of vandalism and wife assault; and (e) cause William McNeil, Manager of said Celtic Football Club, to lock himself in a dressing room with the players of Celtic Football Club where he committed certain unknown acts on said players, all thereby placing the continued livlihood of said William McNeil in jeopardy and did thereby commit a breach of the peace.

Procurator-Fiscal Depute

The Court grants Warrant to apprehend the said Accused and grants warrant to search the person, dwellinghouse and repositories of sais Accused and any place where they may be found and to take possession of the property mentioned or referred to in the Complaint and all articles and docuements likely to afford evidence of guilt or of guilty participa-tion.

Sheriff

Follow, Follow

You're supposed to be at home

Anyone who doubted City as the number one supported team in Manchester should have been at the 'derby'. As the Blues' second team blasted in three goals in the last four minutes. I was amazed to look around the jam-packed main stand to see practically every seat was occupied by ecstatic City fans.

You could tell something special was in the air when queues stretched three deep, 70 yards back from the **one** turn-stile for paying adults, while the **three** turnstiles for United season ticket/membership card holders were more or less redundant.

When the Reds went 3-1 up I put the near silence down to it only being a reserve game and Reds fans apathy to such 'trivial' matters. .But when Trevor Morley headed one back I saw it was because their fans were embarrassingly in the minority.

The true devastating contrast in support was only seen when Moulden (the best taker of chances in football) hit an equaliser and a dramatic winner in injury time.

It was like the North Stand at Maine Road - a thick mass of celebrating Blues and blow up bananas and various beasts. It was the fourth game in five days that a City team had played (including two league and an F.A. Youth Cup Match) and it showed that Blues' fans' appetite for watching their club's representatives is unquenchable. What other club can boast taking an away ground for a reserve match?

One Blue joker quipped that the United contingent was so low because only Manchester Reds watch the reserves - but surely there are more than a few dozen Reds in Manchester, aren't there?

The scenes equalled Stoke away this **year**, the last game in Division one against West Ham and the 20,000 crowd for the F.A. Youth Cup winning match, three years ago and further proved the feeling fans have for City is very special indeed.

Blue Print

LIVING IN THE PAST

NEWBOY David Rennie salvaged a crucial point for a Leeds side fighting for its First Division life.

Congratulations to the Sunday Mirror, the only newspaper which still keeps us informed on Leeds' rather unsuccessful battle for First Division survival. In what may be a world exclusive City Gent can now reveal that Super Leeds were relegated in 1982...

City Gent

A SOAP OPERA FROM BURSLEM

Last week everybody's favourite losers PORT VALE crashed out of the Sherpa Van Trophy, thrashed 5-1 by WOLVES. It would seem to any normal fan that The Vale had blown their chance of any silver ware this season. There are however rumours that the top brass at Vale Park are planning a masterstroke in their quest for glory. PORT VALE are to ask the Welsh FA for permission to enter the Welsh Cup in place of SHREWSBURY TOWN who were expelled from the competition for fielding an ineligible player in the First Round. How can The Vale expect to pull off this daring stunt ? Well it seems that they have managed to convince the Welsh FA that PORT VALE is in fact a small run-down ghetto type mining village situated between PORT TALBOT and EBBW VALE. Simple but brilliant. Once accepted they will be able to take on mighty opponents such as Llandudno Athletic, Pontypool Rovers or even the famous Llanfairpwllgwyngyllgogerychwyrndrobwllllantysiliogogogoch United, (fit that one on your electronic scoreboard smartarses). To further help their cause, manager John 'boyo' Rudge and his assistant Mike 'yacki-dar' Pejic have enrolled their players into a Welsh Language class at nightschool. Already some of the team have made remarkable progress, picking up words and phrases such as "Max Boyce","Cardiff Arms Park" and "Rhyl". Unfortunatley some of the players like Bob Hazell and Ron Futcher have still to master the English Language before tackling really big words like Swansea etc... On the subject of Wales, why don't The Vale take up rugby ? They couldn't possibly be bigger failures at that than they have been at football in the last 112 years.

The Oatcake

RIVALS

Just Another Wednesd

PROPHESY

THE GUARDIAN
Monday January 16 1989

Bristol Rovers 1
Sheffield United 1

A nice day for non-Leaguers

BOYCOTT

Dear NTV,

Never mind a boycott to give the Celtic Board a kick up the botty for what amounts to mere incompetence. What about boycotting a fixture for a much more serious issue?

It has long been my belief that Celtic supporters should never dignify the Rangers sectarian football club by their presence within Ibrox. To hand money over their turnstiles is a direct contribution to the coffers of sectarianism.

I am infuriated at the way the popular press routinely print the three yearly press release from Ibrox stating that players from now on will be signed on merit alone. Indeed I am angry at the way CFC by their presence at Ibrox pay little heed to this on-going restriction of human rights. The policy seems to be that if you don't talk about it then the whole issue will sort itself out.

I'd rather see Celtic forfeit the points at Ibrox than debase the spirit of a game in which a man's ability should be all that matters.

One final point. I actually welcome the arrival of David Murray at Ibrox. Hopefully he will relegate Rangers' 114 years of dishonour to the past and do something about their medieval signing policies.

Yours faithfully,

JOHN DOCHERTY,
Thornhill
(An atheist with a soft spot for Quakers)

Not The View

A to Z of
Blunderland

A   is for *Ashurst*. A man who collected a fortune from Corals in 1985 when his relegation and Milk Cup losers double came up.

B   is for *Billy Whitehurst*. A bricklayer who collects traffic endorsements.

C   is for *Claudio Marangoni*. The most successful Argentian export since Galtieri took his lads to the Falklands for a short holiday.

D   is for *Durban*. A man with so much to offer football, he now runs a tennis centre in Shropshire.

E   is for *England International*. Before Nick Pickering played against Australia in 1983, the last time a Sunderland player appeared for England was in 1976.

F   is for *Fans*. True Sunderland fans can easily be spotted as they appear only at Roker when it is sunny, there's no wind, it's a local derby and they are in the top half of the division, i.e. never!

G   is for *Gillingham*. A 'top class' footballing outfit who deserve a Magpie Merit Award for finally condemning Sunderland to the 3rd Division.

H   is for *Hartlepool*. A tiny obstacle in the way of Denis Smith's drive to Wembley in his Sherpa van.

I   is for *Ian Botham*. Now recovering from his back operation, he strict orders to take it easy and not get over-excited. He purchased a season ticket for Roker.

J   is for *Joker Park*. A piggery just north of the river Wear.

K   is for *Knighton*. A man who got the sack for 'only' getting finish 17th in the 1st Division. So badly had standards slip

L   is for *Local Derby*. Although this used to mean a trip to St. mackem few, in future it is more likely to mean a trip to St. or the Victoria Ground.

M   is for *McMenemy*. If you put a self-confessed Newcastle fan in at Sunderland, just what do you expect.

N   is for *Nick Pickering*. A man who was so desperate to leave Sun he preferred to move and live in a toilet (well actually, it was Co

O   is for *Own Goal*. Who can forget Gordon Chisholm's classic whic the '85 Milk Cup to East Anglia?

P   is for *Pledge*. Big Lawrie made one, "I'll get this club into the play-

Q   is for *Questionable*. As in 'Sunderland are a sleeping giant'. Or, less questionably, 'Sunderland are a pile of wombat droppings'.

R   is for *Roker Roar*. However, due to the tightening-up of the Trade Description Act, this has now been reclassified, (see W).

S   is for *Sunderland F.C.* I emphasise the F.C. as a friend of mine thou they were called 'Sunderland Nil'.

T   is for *Third Division*. This is where the club found its level, where the manager belongs and is a lot more than their fan deserves.

U   is for *Ugly*. Of course, we are talking about Eric Gates, the Goblin King himself. A man so hideous that even Peter Beardsley refused to appear in the same Panini sticker album.

V   is for *Vauxhall Conference*. This was McMenemy's aim until his crusade was cruelly stopped in its tracks.

W   is for *Wearside Whine*.

X   is for *X-Rays*. These are unnecessary as Sunderland's promotion hopes are clearly transparent.

Y   is for *Yo-Yo*. And until Division 2.5 is invented, Sunderland will continue to do so between Divisions 2 and 3.

Z   is for *Zealot*. Defined in the dictionary as a fanatical enthusiast. Quite what this has to do with Sunderland beats me.

John Scorfield

The Mag

When Saturday Comes

The Half Decent FOOTBALL Magazine

February 1989 No. 24

50p

Rangers Shares Crash

It's 3-0 to Hamilton, boss. What do you want to do?

Sell! Sell!

Celtic's Maestro

Lions Lior

COLIN SUGGET'S IDEA, WEAR OUR SHIRTS BACK TO FRONT AND IT LOOKS LIKE WE'RE ATTACHING

The Mag

When Saturday Comes

The Half Decent FOOTBALL Magazine

January 1989 No. 23

50p

Moynihan: My Message to Fans

Go bell-ringing instead.

Sounds like the death-knell for football.

INSIDE

Orient Expressed

Potteries Pair

Sublime Subbuteo

Road to Albania

MAKING THE STORY FIT THE HEADLINE

The Final Hurdle

Isn't it amazing how, when an established Glasgow-born player signs for either Celtic or Rangers, the tabloid press carry the all-too predictable quotes about him fulfilling a life-long ambition signing for the club he (so we are expected to believe) actively supported from the terracings as a boy.

This happened last season following the big-money transfers of Joe Miller from Aberdeen and Ian Ferguson from St Mirren. Spotty Joe informed us "It's a dream come true, I've always been a Celtic supporter" (translation : "I'm a Catholic"). And while Ferguson was involved in his shameful attempts (ably supported by the Daily Record) to get away from Love Street only months after signing a long-term contract, he stated publicly "I'd love to play for Rangers" (translation : "I'm a Protestant")

As these players were still teenagers, to some extent their comments could have been put down to youthful exuberance. No such excuses are possible, however, in respect of Alan Rough and Andy Gray, two experienced internationals, well into their thirties, who ought to have known better (and surely do). When Rough joined Celtic in July it was, we were reliably informed by the media, the realisation of his "life-long ambition to play for Celtic". Oh yeah, since when ? All those years playing for Partick Thistle, Hibs and Scotland – and not a word of it. Bullshit.

Then last month when Gray continued the downward spiral of his career by joining Rangers the stunning truth was revealed – he had always had an ambition to play for the Ibrox club. More bullshit. Cast your mind back to his free-scoring spell at Tannadice in the 70s and indeed during the subsequent 13 years which he has spent in England; how often have you read, even in the Daily Record, of his family's great Rangers 'tradition' or Andy's burning desire to pull on the infamous blue jersey? Me neither.

Had that really been the driving force throughout his career, and the same goes for Rough, you can be sure the Glasgow-based media, normally only too obliging in their attempts to reinforce not just the Old Firm but the West of Scotland religious stereotyping on which it thrives, would have lost no opportunity to highlight that 'fact'.

That they failed to do so confirms that neither Rough nor Gray felt particularly strongly about the green or the blue – until the priority became an eye-catching headline (suitably rewarded) to sell newspapers. It was fiction – but what the hell, why let the facts get in the way of a good story ?

A United fan prepares to enter the Tannadice Street toilets

THE JAKARTA POST

And Smith Must Score!

Newcastle closes gap on Arsenal with 2-0 victory

Standings							
Arsenal	30	17	8	5	58	31	59
Norwich	29	16	8	5	42	30	56
Liverpool	28	14	9	5	46	22	51
Millwall	30	14	8	8	43	33	50
Forest	29	12	12	5	43	30	48
Coventry	31	12	10	9	39	32	46
United	28	11	10	7	37	23	43
Derby	28	12	6	10	31	27	42
Wimbledon	28	12	6	10	34	32	42
Tottenham	31	10	11	10	45	42	41
Everton	29	9	11	9	36	35	38
QPR	30	9	10	11	30	26	37
Middles-brough							
Wednesday	30	8	9	13	35	48	33
Aston Villa	30	8	9	13	26	40	33
Charlton	3	8	10	14	35	46	31
Luton	30	6	12	12	33	45	30
Southamp-ton	30	7	9	14	29	42	30
Newcastle	29	6	11	12	41	56	29
West Ham	30	7	5	15	29	50	26
	27	5	7	15	22	44	22

KEEP TAKING THE TABLOIDS!

When the announcement of the appointment of the Greatest Manager the Would Has Ever Known was broken on October 28th the Street of Shame and the Wapping Liars rubbed their hands with vigorous glee. For here in front of them was an almost perfect recipe for almost certain failure in the ingredients of further rumour spreading and back page filling delight. (Wide boy and Cockney with inflated reputation given huge and expensive ship to steer to Promised Land.) In an age of hopeless and unashamed admiration toward these truly magnificent periodicals we proudly present you, dear reader, with your very own "pull-out-and-keep-glossy-colour-supplement", which fondly chronicles The Vegetable was hailed as The Messiah, **some** of the football players these journalists of great esteem proudly notified us (as though peering into their "gospel troof guv" crystal balls) would be filling those lillywhite shirts come August 27th, long before even El Veg knew 'imself!

TEL: I'M NOT CASH CRAZY

PUSH OFF TEL!

You won't get Pally with me, says Rioch

SPURS IN BUTCHER BID

TEL'S SPANISH SWOOP

Sunsport exclusive

COME HOME GLENN

Kingpin John

Venables wants Leeds star Sheridan

Spurs go for £1m GREAVSIE

TEL'S FOR £1m LATIN

Francescoli is target

MR MONEY

£2

THE PRESS

TRIBUTE TO WIMBLEDON

from the OBSERVER

It has to be said that Wimbledon have earned no more than the right to be outclassed by Liverpool in the final.
10 April 1988 (Following Wimbledon's semi-final win).

The fish-and-chip club from South London .... bone, muscle and running about like headless chickens .... it's 'up yours' football ....
8 May 1988 (Cup Final preview of Wimbledon).

WIMBLEDON'S WEMBLEY WONDERS !
15 May 1988 (Cup Final match report).

Just Another Wednesday

GS SWOOP BY TEL

Spurs boss to splash £450,000 on old pal

EL £½M SWOOP FOR KE

SPURS LINE UP SANSOM

BIG NORM

In the words of Shakespeare himself:
"It is a tale full of sound and fury, signifying..... NOTHING."
or, to put it in a late 80's context:
"Don't believe (don't believe) don't believe der HYPE!!!"

The Spur

FACE IN THE CROWD

On a dismal November night last year, 3756 genuine supporters turned out to watch Sheffield Wednesday play Bournemouth. Those 3756 supporters made history as comprising the lowest ever gate at Hillsborough for a first class match.

As a reward for their loyalty, we have taken a photograph of the crowd and randomly circled one of the spectators. If the lucky lady will come forward we will be delighted to present her with the £5 prize.

Just Another Wednesday

WHAT A DIFFERENCE A MONTH MAKES

City's infamous inconsistency also afflicts those who are paid to watch them.

Saturday, February 4, 1989

PETER GARDNER'S Maine Road Scene 17

Mel must spend a million
Only way for City to go up

Saturday, March 4, 1989 PF

PETER GARDNER'S Maine Road Scene 17

City can shelve £1m splash
Machin has the players

Blue Print

FOOTBALL JOURNALISTS: IS EUTHANASIA THE ANSWER? (Part 1)

What is green in Sheffield, pink in Brum extinct in London and only seen by Man United fans after a Red victory?

Not Yet? Call yerself street-wise, huh?

Then picture this scene - a nervous gathering of urchins, teenagers and wrinklies shuffled around on the pavement, silhouetted against the shafts of light escaping through the open door of the newsagents. Inside the shop more people are milling around expectantly. Yes, if the kids were old enough you would think that their anxious pacing up and down signified an imminent delivery.

Oh, but it does! Slow aren't yer?

Suddenly, a screech of brakes and everyone stiffens to gawp as one man, past the lamp-post to the street corner. Almost before the van stops, Helpful Herbert has caught the string bound bundle chucked out by the drivers mate and is making towards the shop. He pushes through us as the van roars off, and we all turn and follow him inside like a pied piper, our small change at the ready.

You martian or what?

The newsagent cuts the string. His entire family are on parade now, strung out across the whole width of the counter. Each of them takes half a dozen or so and we fan out accordingly, proffer the exact money, take one and turn away, all in the same movement. No words are spoken; no words are needed.

How was the lobotomy?

Outside the kids are scanning the thing by the light of the doorway, running their eyes down great long lists of names and numbers while doing high speed calculations. You push out past then into the darkness, taking care to manipulate the 'Results & Tables' page so as to snatch a quick glance of it as you pass under the first lamp post.

The Saturday night Sports paper, whether pink, blue, green or just plain white is the unsung centrepiece of this weekly ritual shared by all of us outside London. Can you grasp how our Cockney Brethren get by without those endearing hyped up headlines - "Blues blast the Brummies","Sharp jab for Everton" Chirpy Canaries give Reds the Bird" and other gems of journalistic excellence? Even if we do read them for pure information rather than literary merit where else could a goalkeeper's failed clearance produce the headline "Farnworth's Leg Show Punished" or was the Manchester Pink suggesting something else about Bury's man between the sticks?

LOADSAMONEY

Regular away fans will be familiar with the syndicated columns in these papers. If you are the manager of Unileverton Spurasre (yes I'm determined to repeat that phrase until it catches on) a relatively well known ex-player, current 'star' or name referee, it can be a nice little earner to have your ghosted article syndicated to sports papers from Southampton to Sunderland. The local rag will alter a paragraph here and there to give a local flavour, so it is basically like after dinner speaking without having to shift your butt: Howard Kendall seems to do very nicely out of this line without even being in the country.

ROBBED 0-5

The real eye opener into the nether world of unashamed parochialism comes when you pick up the local rag in the away town within an hour or so of having personally witnessed something completely and utterly different from what passes as a report on the same match. These hacks are clearly writing for a particular market,and what might have happened on the pitch just doesn't enter into it. Your team could have won 5-0 at a canter, but you'll likely as not pick up a 'we wuz robbed' blow-by-blow job in which your striker's screamer from 25 yards goes down as a defensive mix up and the other 4 read like breakaways because only the home players' antics rate more than a passing mention.

Football ECHO

BOWLS

These reports are there most distorted whenever the home team leaks goals in the final 25 minutes, because of the production schedules which seem to defy the laws of time. Column after column dedicated to the mind numbing first half, in which the only 2 shots came from your team , are regurgitated in print now as if your lads never got over the halfway line in the 45 minutes, and just before the match reports disappear into a Bowls league table. the half time 0-0 score spans the column in bold dark typeface like some kind of absolute, final statement. Maybe - maybe not - the report is continued on the back page and so you flip over to the tiny paragraphette under the name of the team you thrashed.

THE BALLAD OF WITTON ALBION

Our fame has spread for miles around
We play at the Central Ground
Cups and trophies we will clinch 'em
When we move to our new purpose built stadium at Wincham

Points and goals we'll surely harvest
with the delicate touch of Tony Jarvis
He's the man who does inspire
and come to think of it so does Reg McGuire
After the match we go home happily bedwards
to dream of goals scored by Mark Edwards
Players of reknown we've certainly got 'em
Like John Brown, Nigel Deeley, Graham Ford and Paul Higginbotham

And who could forget our player-coach
even though nothing rhymes with John Davison

Bishop 3-1

BOILS

There on the back page you find the absolute minimum of grudging, frequently misspelt recognition of the eventual outcome, something like- "Yet more home attacks came to nothing and tricky winger Archangel's cross was punched out by the visitor's keeper Titarse, from which BULL broke away to score. BOIL grabbed his second after 71 minutes and PHORN added a third with 10 minutes left. PORN & BILE both scored again before the end."

TUNNEL VISION

Finally your sense of unreality is compounded by the inside page of this strange, alien propaganda sheet. There you find a cheery gossipy article by the only decent player in the team your side has just thrashed, in which he swears that he can see the light at the end of the tunnel and looks forward to the match you have just watched. He informs the reader's that all the lads are behind the Boss who was sacked in between the article having been ghosted and the game.

It's almost as much fun as reading this stuff as it is ringing their Clubcall from work on the Monday

The Double Agent

Rodney, Rodney

The Final Hurdle

WEDNESDAY July 12

Daily Rangers

22p   FORWARD WITH SCOTLAND

GERS STAR CATCHES BAD COLD

BUTCHER IN SNIFFLE SENSATION   EXCLUSIVE

Ibrox was rocked to its foundations yesterday when it became known that superstar Terry Butcher may miss tomorrow's vital photo session - due to a heavy cold.

SASH

A grim-faced Graeme Souness, Ibrox supremo, or God, refused to comment as he rushed out of the Bluenose Room. But his dogsbody, Walter Smith, delivered the shattering news all Scotland had dreaded. In a one-sentence press release he stated "Tel has a sore throat and a blocked nose, but at the end of the day the lads will just have to do the photo business without him".

MASON

Smith would not be drawn on reports that Rangers will be scouring the world for a replacement, adding "We have only £5m to spend by Xmas". Asked (though not by this paper) if the new signing would be a Catholic, he stormed out muttering something about 'trick questions' 'policy' and 'no ecumenism'.

LODGE

Poor Tel is confined to bed in his £1m mansion and the other players want the photo call postponed. Richard Gough, an expert on squirming out of contracts, and Andy Gray, not sure why he is there at all, (continued on back page)

GET UP TO THE MINUTE INFO ON TERRY'S COLD BY CALLING THE RANGERS HUNLINE ON 0898 1690

calls will be charged at an exorbitant rate

UNITED IN CUP TRIUMPH

Dundee United won the European Cup Winners Cup last night

WHERE ARE THEY NOW?

The second in an extremely short series which looks at long forgotten people, or in this case a long forgotten newspaper, with a past connection with Queens Park Rangers.

2) The London Daily News:

THE LONDON DAILY NEWS

All Rangers fans who have ever stood, or sat even, at Oxfords Manor Ground will no doubt mourn the passing of Robert Maxwells oh so caring London Daily News. It will of course always be remembered as one of the newspapers that offered two season tickets, to Fulham Park Rangers, in a prize competition. Alas, the paper is now as dead as another of Maxwells brainchilds — Thames Valley Royals. Queens Park Rangers however are still going strong. As Jimmy Greaves might say "It's a funny old game'.

A Kick Up The Rs

STOP PRESS

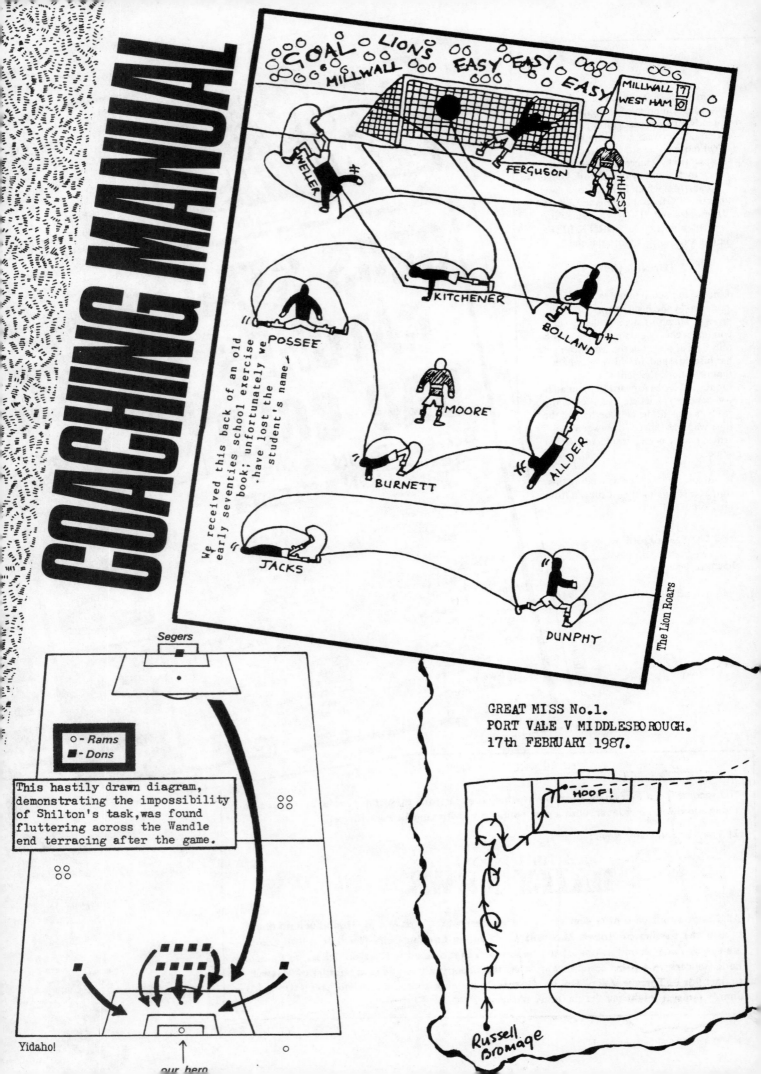

THE WEMBLEY WAY?

Is it surprising that England never receives the chance to hold a major international sporting event of any description when our stadia are decayed and outdated? Wembley as part of 'improvement work' is to have its capacity reduced to 86,000 when, yes you've guessed it, executive boxes are to be installed later this year. Since cup ties began we have heard tales of lifelong fans being unable to get tickets for the final because only 25,000 are made available to each club.

Surely an increase in capacity is what's needed not a reduction, countries which are supposedly among the world's bankrupt (Mexico, Brazil etc) have some of the biggest and most impressive grounds in the world so why are we lumberd with Wembley?

If Manchester does manage to win the vote for the 1996 Olympics then hopefully we'll have a place, not only more central to fans from all over the country, but somewhere which people will enjoy going to. Up until then fans of teams likely to go to 'That Hallowed Stadium' will have to keep hoping that Wimbledon or Charlton qualify with them for the final to stand a chance of getting in.

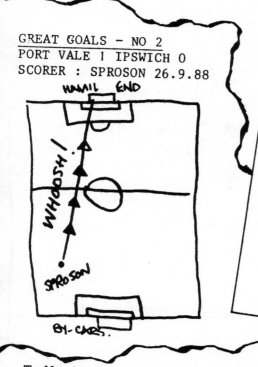

GREAT GOALS - NO 2
PORT VALE 1 IPSWICH 0
SCORER : SPROSON 26.9.88

HAMIL END

WHOOSH!

SPROSON

BY-CARS.

The Memoirs of Seth Bottomley

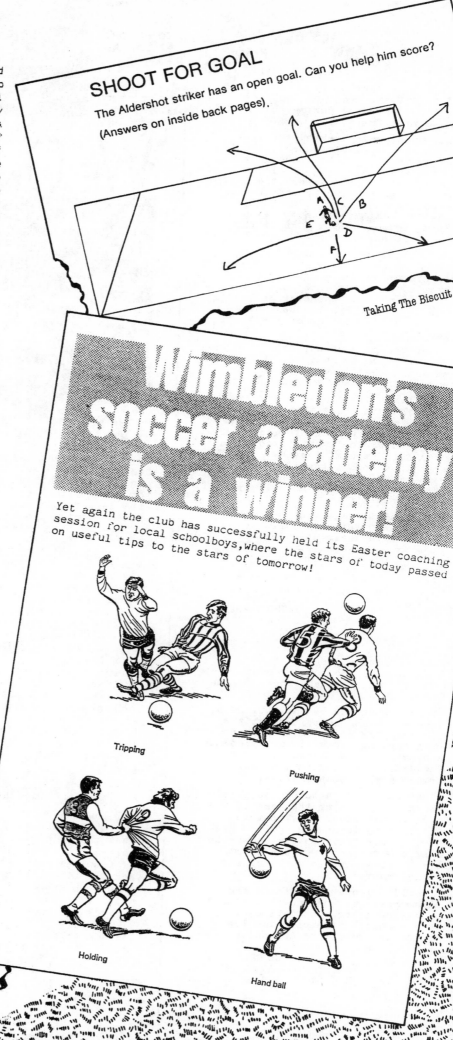

SHOOT FOR GOAL

The Aldershot striker has an open goal. Can you help him score?

(Answers on inside back pages).

Taking The Biscuit

Wimbledon's soccer academy is a winner!

Yet again the club has successfully held its Easter coaching session for local schoolboys, where the stars of today passed on useful tips to the stars of tomorrow!

Tripping

Pushing

Holding

Hand ball

Yidaho!

Dear Orientear,

I am writing about an incident which took place during the first game with Enfield.

I was standing behind the goal with the other O's supporters. I began thinking that although the O's are a small team, at least we have what I thought were the best behaved supporters around. Even when the team is playing badly one doesn't have to worry about being involved in a fight with opposite supporters.

Alas, all my thoughts of being proud of being an O's fan turned to dismay when a small group started chanting "only white team in London", and whenever Enfield's two black players touched the ball, chants went up of "f*** off you black bastard."

When the genuine supporters began to tell them to shut up, the reply was: "You won't say that when some nigger takes your mother's bag."

I think the thing that annoyed me the most was that a few yards away stood a couple of black O's fans who couldn't have been older than 12. How must they have felt? If either one of those youngsters reads this letter, the only thing I can say is we are not all like that here.

My final message goes out to the animals who think they are being clever with their chanting: Go away. We don't want you at Leyton Stadium.

I would like to hear the views of genuine supporters on the subject.

ANDREW FOLEY
LONDON
NW1.

Dear Orientear,

I am writing about two recent matches. and the behaviour of some Orient fans.

I was sickened by the actions of some so-called supporters at the Enfield game on November 20. who were hurling abuse at our opponents' 2 black players. I was so angry, I ended up getting into a heated argument with these idiots.

What can we do about these people who are disgracing the name of the club we all love? One possible solution is to ask the police present to use their powers under the Public Order Act 1986 and eject/arrest these people for inciting racial hatred.

I would welcome suggestions from other readers. and would recommend a meeting of representatives from this magazine, the club and the police to see how we can solve this problem.

JOHN QUIRKE
LEYTONSTONE
E11.

Leyton Orientear

'WE ONLY SING WH

SHANKLY LIVES FOREVER

The Kop...It's all gone quiet over there.

Many of the bad points I make about the Kop here are common to all football crowds, a few are unfortunately unique to this home terracing. Many of the points will only refer to the middle third of the Kop, and perhaps the lesser half of this, but this is where most of the "noise" comes from.

I had been told, like everyone else, of the legend that was 'The Kop', so when I first went to Anfield I made straight for the most famous part of the ground. I wanted to savour the great atmosphere at the centre of the Kop, the crowd surges, the endless defeaning chanting, striking fear into all opposing teams. I wanted to stand amongst one of the most intelligent, fair minded and humourous crowds to be found at any football ground.

Something was wrong, it would have been an effort to find any atmosphere to talk of, and far worse than that, a perverse sense of humour, and often fair minded only when Liverpool were winning. Worse of all, racism was abundant, I was not aware that I was to expect this more in Liverpool than in many other places.

Eventually I became too frustrated with the constant pushing, and the lie that this was something special. (I'm also dead short and couldn't see anything). I moved to the left, near the back, there's plenty of room and a good view, now I observe the centre of the Kop, and do not associate myself with it. So what observations have I made?

UGLY RACISM

You'd have thought that the arrival of John Barnes would at least shut up the racists (and get rid of those that really meant it), but even if some people stopped going, others still thought it funny, and of course lots of mindless idiots still join in. My case in point, this season, Liverpool v Newcastle United, a young Brazilian, Francisco Ernandi Lima da Silva, scores in front of the Kop, he gestures to the Kop, Johnny Barnes is injured, so he's not playing, and the chanting starts, 'You Black ...I wonder if his parents weren't married, anyway, how Barnes felt sitting in the main stand I don't know, I guess Mirandinha was confused, he must surely be the lightest 'black' person ever to appear at Anfield.

ISM
EN WE'RE WINN

If Mirandinha is given stick for the darkness of his skin, then Barnes is really in for a hard time isn't he. Probably not, but only because he's wearing a **Liverpool** shirt. Most of these racists are fickle and inconsistent - part timers. They can be silenced, so don't just stand there, say something.

All mankind are equal. Racism is sick and unfunny, the racist near you how wrong they are, and you should get through. If the Kop becomes intelligent and fair minded about this one I shall be impressed.

What's in and what's out this season.

In - Promotion
In - The West
In - Support
In - Friendly Rivalry
In - Winning
In - Chelsea/Rangers away shirts
In - Robbo
In - Campbell
In - Fanzines
In - Mirror/Mail
In - Coke/Mineral Water
In - New Balance/Nike Air trainers
In - Two jumpers
In - Dark socks
In - Middx Charity Cup
In - Haircuts
In - Solar watches
In - Zin TVs
In - Goals for
In - BBC football

In - Ian Botham
In - Chucklevision
In - News of the World
In - Satellite TV
In - Burger King
In - Labour candidate for Lewisham East

Out - Relegation
Out - The Shed
Out - Abuse
Out - Trouble
Out - Losing
Out - Home shirts
Out - Hazard
Out - Hollins
Out - Programmes (home)
Out - Sun/Star
Out - Booze
Out - Basketball boots/HiTec
Out - Jackets
Out - White pairs
Out - Simod Cup
Out - Long hair
Out - Earrings
Out - Walkmans
Out - Goals against
Out - ITV

Out - Emlyn Hughes
Out - Wide awake Club
Out - Sunday Sport
Out - Videos
Out - McDonalds
Out - Moynihan

The Red Card

ACTING BADLY

Seeing as 1 got a rather gut-turning picture I thought I'd go into detail on a point that could go in the yet more examples bit. Millwall played some decent stuff at Anfield, and picked up a couple of nasty injuries, an example is on your right. How did the Kop act when Ian Dawes lay injured shortly before being carried off? Well I may (not) surprise you that it wasn't too clever. Or is "Who's the actor in the blue?" funny?

Could Liverpool lose their fair play title?

'MUNICH'

I'll probably do a whole article about this in the next Issue, but for now...I'm told this chant only began about 10 years ago, and from my experience I hope it has gone through a peak. It goes beyond having a go at the fans of one of the teams you want Liverpool to beat the most. How would someone feel if they'd lost a close relative in the Zeebrugge disaster, and someone came up and started telling jokes about second hand lorries falling off the backs of ferries.

When Sunday Comes

RACISM

BLUE - THE ONLY COLOUR THAT MATTERS

The creative wing and midfield play of Mark Walters since he signed from Aston Villa has graced every pitch he has played on north of the border.

Unfortunately the fact that he's black has led sizeable sections of morons in other clubs to overlook his skills. His reception at Parkhead and Tynecastle put back their efforts to somehow portray themselves as "progressive" or "family" clubs. In marked contrast Rangers fans have given Mark tremendous support in face of the hostility and sickening racism that he's been subjected to. If a handful of nazis have stopped going to the Stadium then that's great - we're better off without such scum soiling the club.

We don't claim that Rangers fans are angels, if another team had signed a black man then no doubt a minority would have disgraced us by their behaviour - no doubt "inspired", like the Tims and the Jam Tarts, by the juvenile antics of racist clubs in England. Indeed, when we played Chelsea and Ajax a couple of coloured guys came in for abuse - simply due to ignorance and copy-cat behaviour.

Some rabid Tims, like ex-Chelsea player Pat Nevin, displayed their usual paranoia over the Gers and claimed that the abuse "rang around the park" - CRAP. The only place it rang around was in the thick empty heads of the doughballs stupid enough to believe themselves better than another person because of their colour. The vast majority of supporters sat, or stood, embarrassed, silent and angry - helpless to counter the rubbish.

It's good to see that Mark's presence has encoraged many more members of Glasgow's minority communities to come along and support the team. Even before he arrived a poll showed that 80% were Gers fans. They're more than welcome.

When Mark eventually leaves we hope that his stay will have ensured that abuse from the stands and terraces populated by Rangers fans will be directed against players because of their lack of skill and not their colour.

Follow, Follow

RACISM

Why do you taunt black players ?

White people who reveal the offensive side of their nature when their eyes behold black players on the pitch fall into 2 categories :-

Overt racists who have a built in hatred and fear of non-whites

People who also taunt the plumper / balder / lankier etc players, managers, and physios, but deny they are racists.

I have no idea what to do about the racists, people who feel happy in that philosophy. I certainly wouldn't advocate the measures they'd doubtless bring to bear on their target group. I would ask, however, that they keep quiet at the footy, because their crap invariably inspires the black opponents and as a result we get beat. However, most people (I hope) are not racist and wouldn't want their behavoir to indicate in anyway that they might be. When they scream " Oo oo oo " when a " jungle bunny" or " darkie " gets the ball it's just the same as when they chant " you bald bastard " at the ref, or scream " fatty " at Paul Gasgoine, and is therefore acceptable (some would say it's all unacceptable, but that's not my point). When I hear someone near me in the River End shout " when the coon gets the ball he'll try to get the milk out " it has nothing to do with banter designed to put the opponents off and everything to do with a society that is historically, and presently horrific- ally racist. Being born black means that in recent history you have/could have :

Been colonized, having your own culture eroded in your own country

Been separated from your family, loved ones, community by the colonial govenors

Been enslaved to serve the new rulers, and shipped abroad like cattle with scant regard whether you live or die

Or more recently :-

Invited to a country (Britain) which needs your labour, discovering when you get there that that means all the shit jobs that the indigenous white population doesn't want

Showed into ghettos in the most run down of our inner cities, and rejected by the rest of the working class

Subjected to abuse when you walk the street, harrassment, intimidation, etc Victims of facist attacks which could mean beatings, firebombings ...

Victim of economic policies which try to force your family ' back to where they came from ' even though you are probably the 3rd generation to be born here and have British Citizenship

That when you maybe succeed in life (if the status of professional footballer and wealth is success) you are subject to the sort of barracking that revives that history, that draws on it, that reinforces it, that keeps you inferior because of the colour of your skin.

Every time you shout or express (or perhaps even think) " nigger ", you support that disgraceful history and scenario that is now. Do you really want that ? It could easily be you.

Trevor.

SNAPPY NOEL

Leeds Other Paper recently interviewed Noel Blake, the hero at the heart of our defence.

LOP: Leeds United are making some progress under Howard Wilkinson. Did the managerial uncertainty create problems for the players?
NB: Ever since I've been here with the old manager, you came in, picked up the papers and saw that the manager's going to get the sack. This didn't bring stability from the players' point of view. If the manager does go and someone new comes you think 'Will he want you?' Especially in my position, centre half, you don't know whether he fancies a footballing centre half as against a stopper, I'm a stopper. So far he's been inclined to play my style of centre half. We're a long way from the top but the manager has brought in fresh blood and turned things over, put us on the right lines.
LOP: Where did you start in football?
NB: At Aston Villa. I was born in Jamaica and came to Birmingham at the age of nine. When I signed pro, at the age of seventeen and played my first League game a few months later, I felt if I never did another thing in my life I'd die happy because I'd achieved my ambition. It's my job, my hobby, I wanted to do it and I did it. After Villa I played for Birmingham City before spending four years with Portsmouth. There every game was a pressure game, similar to Leeds in many respects, if we won everyone was happy, if we lost - terrible.
LOP: Did you have any doubts about joining Leeds United?
NB: No. I've said this in the past and a lot of people have questioned why I say 'No'. Obviously I know about the reputation of Leeds and their fans, racial abuse and what have you. As a visiting player I had stick which Mr. Silver the Leeds chairman very nicely wrote and apologised for.

I spoke to Terry Connor, a black lad who used to be here before coming to Portsmouth.

He said 'Just get up there, once you put a white shirt on in their eyes as it were you're a god'.

You do get racial abuse and the vindictive side of it is very hard.

I experienced something at Portsmouth which I wished never to experience. I had just moved down from Birmingham, the first time I left home and we were expecting our second child. I found it very hard to settle. One of the reasons was the home crowd giving constant abuse about your colour, not all but a certain section. I'm not kidding it was constant abuse. It hurt me so much at the time because I was playing for them, I was trying to win games for them. That is something I will personally never forget. Even to the extent that I once went to pick up a ball from the touchline, appealing to the linesman for the throw, when a Portsmouth steward turned and said 'It's their ball you black so and so.' I just stood and looked. I couldn't believe it. The majority of Pompey fans were great however and the Chairman stood by us. When I threatened to walk out saying 'I can't handle this' he said he'd buy eleven black players if he needed to. In the end I thought 'Why give in?' If you run away from it they'll give it to you worse.

You've got to say alright, I'm black, there is no question about that. You've got to stand up and be counted. I fought it and I fought it and in fact I had four good years there, becoming player of the year twice and club captain

LOP: And have your experiences at Portsmouth been reflected here at all?
NB: No, No. Far from it, Leeds supporters have been superb, both on and off the field. Let's not forget that it'll never be 100% here. That element is there on the terraces, we do what we can to stem it but basically we just try to get on with our jobs and play. I'll tell you the typical Leeds United fan is a fanatic, I've played for some clubs which I thought had staunch supporters but these are unbelievable. I have signed a two year contract. I know it's early days but I'm enjoying my football and life here in West Yorkshire. All being well I'd like to finish my career here.

About the racial thing, ever since I've been up here it's been, not thrown at me, but coming up, coming up. I say lets live and let live, whether you're black or white, Chinese or whatever.

Marching Altogether (Anti-racist)

LEEDS UNITED AGAINST RACISM & FASCISM

COMPETITION RESULT ++++++ COMPETITION RESULT ++

Well as expected nobody managed to name all three of the players that Andy Roxburgh is talking to so nobody won Competition A. and we get to keep all the lovely prizes. Three people managed two out of three - Ray Stewart and Billy Kirkwood - but nobody got Steve Nicol who is bending. Somebody has won Andy Roxburghs autograph though (as well as a lifetime subscription to F.U and a bumper bundle of other Fanzines - we might even throw in a T-Shirt). Our top five favourite captions were in descending order

5th... 'Let me introduce you to three of the cast of Neighbours'. Andrew Gardner, Bainsford.
4th... 'Sorry Lads but the Clydebank defence was the best I could do'. Boomer Essiason, Cumbernauld
3rd... 'Aye Boys, three dummy's and not one plays for Dunfermline'. Ian Thomson, Grangemouth.
2nd... 'Come on boss, the England defence wont be that mobile on Saturday'. Willie Sharp, Preston.
1st... 'What do you mean they're not real footballers'. Steve McDonagh, Edinburgh.

Falkirk Unofficial Fanzine

I'll let you know they've all got Fife Cup medals'.

RACISM

The Spur

The A to Z of The Arse

I'm only a poor little . . . . . .

The Spur editorial is committed to Anti-racism so therefore perhaps it is time to put this doctrine into perspective at Spurs. Let's face it, racism is still present here at Spurs as well as in football and society in general. Anti-black racism has always been a focal point of racist controversy in British football, largely due to the fact that there are so many good black players and that they are an undoubted force in the game. Still, however, black people make up a tiny part of football crowds especially considering that many big teams come from Britain's major cities. This must be put down to the fact that large, prominent and noisy areas of football grounds are dominated by young, white, males who have adopted the racist ideologies this group often perpetuates. The simple solution to this problem is as the F.S.A. and many fanzine editorials frequently point out, to break down this dominant group by encouraging children, women, pensioners, handicapped people and all members of society to come to football matches again. This could be simply done for example, offering concessions to these groups at turnstiles, providing wheelchair access points womens toilets and evicting people from grounds for racist, sexist or offensive abuse.

Instead of this, however, the Government and the Football League offer us the 100% membership scheme and the Tottenham board offer us limited access to White Hart Lane due to their own duplicity in demolishing The Shelf terracing. Clearly this will be opposite to the desired effect, discouraging casual and potential new fans from attending games.

One good thing at Tottenham is that collective anti-black racism ('apeing' and banana throwing) has more or less disappeared as, presumably the illogic of taunting visitors' black players when we have our own is obvious (this does not unfortunately apply to individuals and Spurs fans away from home). The same thing has occurred at Arsenal who, to be honest put Spurs to shame with their youth and community programmes. A growing amount of black and Asian supporters mix harmoniously at Highbury and they have even set the precedent of taking two women on a YTS to train them to be football coaches.

By contrast Spurs links with the community are

tenuous to say the least. Scholar excuses the clubs lack of involvement by saying that most Spurs fans don't come from the immediate area. Unfortunately, the board refuse to communicate with, *The Spur*, (us being political subversives) but, for example, I wonder if T.H.PLC are an equal opportunities employer? Either way encouragingly racial harmony at Spurs certainly isn't the boards priority (as are all things that don't necessarily generate revenue). The more keen-eyed amongst us will notice the club photographers insistance on always placing black team members symetrically either side of the goalkeeper in team photos. A minor point perhaps but is it necessary? Chris and Mitch, don't you object to being used as 'objects'', rather than people regardless of skin colour? Most Spurs supporters may well not come from the immediate area but the fact that they're not encouraged to might just have something to do with it. After all we don't all come from Broxborough, Herts.

The most racist supporters I have witnessed are those of Leeds, Everton and Chelsea. The first two are endemic of what I speculatively call the Northern racist problem. With few or no coloured players in their teams when hosting those who do, all the usual vulgar abuse is rife. Leeds fans a few years ago apparently harrassed their own Terry Connor so severely (for taking risks and being adventurous) that he left the club for Brighton and later Portsmouth. Connor, was a born and bred Yorkshireman. Integration such as is beginning at Arsenal and Spurs must be the solution to this problem. John Barnes and Mark Walters have acted as ambassadors for their race in going to teams with no previous history of black players. The attention they have received because of this has provoked criticism of the racist fans and moves to curb them. Hopefully Hilaire and Blake will act in this capacity at Leeds, coupled, I should point out with the clubs admirable policies of leafletting, pressing programme messages from the players and public announcements denouncing the racists. At Leeds, however, a lot may depend on what effect Blake and Hilaire have on the fortunes of the team.

A is for **ARSENAL**, the only Club not to get into the 'First Division on merit. They cheated their way in in 1919.

B is for **BOREDOM**, a traditional and common emotion experienced by those witnessing Arsenal play.

C is for **CUP FINAL**. Arsenal have managed to lose more of these than any other Club: FA Cup; 1927, 1932, 1952, 1972, 1978, 1980 - League Cup; 1968, 1969, 1988 - ECWC; 1980.

D is for **DONKEY**. Some uncharitable people believe the current Arsenal captain is one of this species.

E is for **EUROPE**, an area where Arsenal have achieved little success.

F is for **FOOTBALL LEAGUE MANAGEMENT COMMITTEE**. An organisation from which the current Arsenal Chairman, David Dein, has recently been removed from.

G is for **GRAHAM**, George. While still a player, a young supporter apparently asked George what went through his head as he ran down the wing. He replied, "Nothing really"

H is for **HANDLES**. Arsenal's only trophy this decade didn't have any

I is for **INTERESTING**. Interesting to note that on the fourth of April 1983 (when Arsenal lost a North London derby 0-5) the match ball was sponsored by Lawrence Wisepart.

J is for **JOKE**. Such as Arsenal winning the League title this season.

K is for **KENNY** Sansom...

L is for **LUCKY**. Anyone who is associated with Arsenal generally tend to get upset if you drop this word in the same sentence as the name of their team.

M is for **MOAN**. Some uncharitable people believe that Arsenal do a lot of this when they lose.

N is for **NICHOLAS**, Charlie. A right Charlie!

O is for **ORIFICE**. There is a reference to an orifice in the name, Arsenal.

P is for **PENALTY**. Certain Arsenal players have been known to find it particularly difficult to score from this free shot at all of twelve yards.

Q is for **QUINN**, Niall. Brian Glanville's favourite Arsenal player. The new George Best.

R is for **RIX**, Graham. A great penalty taker for Arsenal on the European stage.

. . . racist

The other team I mentioned earlier, Chelsea, seem to attract the supporters of most fascistic tendencies. Despite the inclusion of Clive Wilson in the team integration off the field is minimal. In fact at Stamford Bridge last season some Chelsea fans found it within themselves to harrass Chris Fairclough while he was marking Wilson. Absurd and offensive. Again the solution must be to perservere with measures such as advocated at Leeds.

While anti-black racism has been exposed and even sometimes condemned by the media, (though the tabloids do tend to advertise it) semitic racism centering on Spurs persists and lingers as a source of offense and embarrassment to me and I suspect many others

Ebony and Ivory, side by side...

also. All the London clubs visit White Hart Lane armed with vulgar anti-semitic ammunition, particularly Arsenal, Chelsea and West Ham. Why Spurs are so inexorably linked with the Jewish community is a slight mystery to me. Only a small percentage of Spurs fans must actually be Jewish, nevertheless the 'Yido' songs' (when Spurs used to sing at home) extend this strange false identity to all Spurs fans. Personally I find it bewildering. "Yido" has become a byword for a Spurs fan and can be casually used in conversation to mean this. For example, at *The Spur*, we have received letters addressed, 'Dear Yid', and I remember amongst many other occasions the cup semi-final 86-87 at Villa Park where the Star of David punctuated the obligatory line of Union Jacks. Quite plainly the acceptability of this racism by both Spurs and visiting fans is truly offensive. Some of the anti-semitic songs brought to White Hart Lane are a disgrace. Because the whole 'Yido', phraseology has become embedded in the fans diction it is rarely condemned, in fact many people it seems are not concerned or even aware of the implications of their language and actions. The television media

never mention it, in a live television match last season John Motson condemned Everton fans for 'apeing' Franz Carr, however, the clearly audible, 'Yido, Yido' chants and taunts stay un-challenged. It appears it is at Tottenham to stay. The Club (meaning the board) obviously pander to the myth/fact(?) that all Spurs fans are Jewish, note the orignal rescheduled Coventry game was deferred to avoid Yom Kippur. I for one would certainly like to see more frequent programme notes or inserts, public announcements and evictions to deter anti-semitism at Spurs and other London grounds.

Worryingly at the pre season game at Upton Park Spurs fans were taunting West Ham fans for the fact that their ground is situated in the heart of East Londons Asian community. The nature of this abuse was similar to the way Spurs fans are often attacked for being situated around the London/ Jewish community. Hooliganism, racism, sexism etc are all social problems and it is as social meeting places that sports grounds play house to these attitudes. Because of the age, sex, race and 'class' of people that it traditionally encourages soccer has become most deeply entrenched in these problems. This group of people are, unfortunately, most prone to extreme degrees of bigotry, false patriatism, violence, drunkeness etc and the vehicle that becomes their identity is their respective football club. The encouragement offered by sections of the media to refer to other nationalities as 'Krauts, Dagos' etc and to values of proud patriatism play a large part in perpetuating these un-sightly values. As stated at the beginning of this article I feel this group needs to be broken down by encouraging everyone to football games.

Football fans must face their responsibility as members of society just as politicians must face the problems violence, drunkeness as social problems not just as footballs'.

I certainly feel it may take a concerted effort to challenge the popular racist attitudes in Britain but any efforts are a start in making British society and British football grounds a pleasant place to be for everyone. Then we would have something to be proud of.

Doug Cheeseman

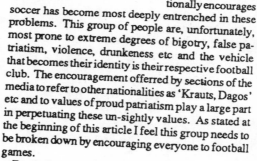

S is for **SOUTH EAST COUNTIES LEAGUE DIVISION ONE**. Well known and natural habitat of ex-Arsenal captains.

T is for **TOTTENHAM HOTSPUR**. A team who have won at Arsenal's home ground, Highbury on more occasions than any other Club.

U is for **UGLY**. Some uncharitable people believe that the current Arsenal captain fits this harsh observation.

V is for **VALENCIA**. Better at taking penalties than Arsenal.

W is for **WOOLWICH**. Despite many of Arsenals' supporters' claim that their team are the Pride of Norf Lunnun, the Club do in fact originate from Woolwich, which (we hate to say it) is nowhere near North London.

X is for **XENOPHON**. Athenian writer (435 - 355 B.C.). Didn't play for Arsenal, but probably took a better penalty than Nigel Winterburn.

Y is for **YORK CITY**, who knocked Arsenal out of the FA Cup in joyous fashion in 1985.

Z is for **ZZZZZZZZZZZZZZZZZZ**

TEN THINGS YOU DIDN'T KNOW ABOUT
albania OR FOREIGNERS ON ALBANIA

I. Albania has a very strict dress code for tourists, and has a history of torturing transvestites.

2. Vllaznia Schkoder is not, in fact, a social disease, but a football team which once went through a whole season without dropping a point.

3. Albanians are appalingly bad spellers, note the following British clubs...
LIDS, ÇELSI, UEST HEM, NJUKESTELL, GLLAZKOU REINXHERS.

4. Despite this, Albanian is an easy language. The word for drink is 'pi'.
So if you're desperate to go just pay 3 and a seventh in their money and Bob's your Uncle.

> The figure of Enver Hoxha is all-sided, giving his work and life the dimensions of an epoch — the most brilliant epoch of our ancient people. He was born and molded as a revolutionary at a time when the country and the people needed a far-sighted leader, loyal to the interests of the nation. Enver

5. Beware Albanian childrens' books!
'C'fare do te jete origjini i tyne?' purports to say 'Did you have a jolly time paying the fare, in a new jet, flying over the Tyne?'
However the true meaning is 'If you come naked into this room, I can interrupt you!'

6. Albanian currency is I00 qindarkes =I LEK, (10.36 LEK =1 pound sterling).

7. The most successful Albanian "treijner" was one Zhenon Gjinali of Dinamo, they won the championship 6 times in 7 years during the 50's.

8. Partisan Tirana once scored 136 goals in 26 games, losing only twice. They still only came second in the league to Dinamo.

9. The fans' favourite song is ...
      "sing uen it's Lenin,
       ui onlli zing uen it'sLenin,
       ui luv our Enver,
       hi's ded, hi'll liv furevver!"

10. There are, of course, thousands of things you didn't know about Albania, so I have tried to bring you the most interesting ones. If you would like to know more (no more) you could visit the Albania shop in London but I'm afraid I can't remember the address. For soccer fans, 'HIstoria e Futbollit' by Skifter Kellici (Shifter Kelly) is an excellent read, especially if you can understand albanian. If you saw Greece vs. England you will know what to expect from the Albania team (so says Bobby Robson).

New facilities for the «17 Nëntori» sports club and the training centre for Albania's national teams are under construction, too.

It was a pleasure for the public of Tirana, Durrës, Gjirokastra to attend those fine performances by the friendly artists from the england team who aroused emotions and won sincere applause. And this is quite natural between two friendly peoples with ancient cultures and traditions.

ALBANIAN DAILY POST
9th. March 1989

The Lad Done Brilliant

Super League Review

IT IS now 10 years since the Football Spectators' Bill came into operation and, with the 'football hooligan' long since relegated to the nation's supermarkets of a Saturday, our top soccer grounds have never been so safe. Now streamlined to twelve clubs, the League has never looked fitter, leaner or more enterprising. So much have things improved that English clubs may even be allowed back into Europe next season.

In this tenth anniversary issue, NICK BROWN looks at how things finished in season 1999-2000, and delves into some of the history behind the new-look League.

FOOTBALL LEAGUE FINAL TABLE 1999-2000

	P	W	D	L	Pts	Av Gate	Highest
1. Liverpool	22	12	6	4	42	7,100	15,021
2. Manchester United	22	9	9	4	36	4,810	6,000
3. Tottenham H.	22	10	5	7	35	10,000	18,200
4. Arsenal	22	9	6	7	33	11,120	20,009
5. West London Utd	22	8	8	6	32	9,900	18,800
6. Everton	22	8	8	6	32	7,900	13,900
7. Birmingham Utd	22	7	8	7	29	6,200	18,002
8. AFC Docklands	22	7	7	8	28	4,002	7,050
9. North East Utd	22	7	6	9	27	2,800	8,000
10. Yorkshire County	22	6	6	10	24	3,050	8,500
11. Nottingham/Derby	22	4	9	9	21	4,500	5,000
12. Lancashire County	22	3	6	13	15	2,050	6,200

CLUB PROFILE

Arsenal: Looked likely to fold in the early 90's, but new Chairman David Evans, formerly with the now-defunct Luton Town, has presided over a spanking refurbishment of Highbury. This is one of the few clubs to maintain a section of terracing in deference to soccer nostalgia. Capacity: 25,000. Admission: 12-seat box £875, 8-seat box £600, Seat £40, Terrace £20.

Birmingham Utd: The Boggles, as they are known to their die-hard fans, play in the gigantic Olympic Stadium where it is hoped the 2012 Games will be played. Capacity: 60,000. Admission: 12-seat box £800, 8-seat box £520; Seat £40, Terrace £20.

AFC Docklands: Based in the former home of Fisher Ahletic, this club has many interesting facilities, but is threatened with closure after an incident last season involving 'supporters' of the now defunct West Ham and Millwall clubs. Capacity 8,000. Admission: 12-seat box £850, 6-seat family box £300.

Everton: A rather old ground, the club freely admits it needs to spend more on boxes and business attractions. Capacity 15,000. Admission: 12-seat box £300, 3-seat box £520, Seats £30 or £20.

Lancashire County: Formed in 1997 from the remnants of Preston, Blackburn, Blackpool, Bolton and Burnley, this club offers superb facilities for any business. This was the first club to run a share-broking service from its executive lounge. Capacity: 8,000. Admission: 12-seat box £650, 8-seat box £400, Seats £35 or £25.

Liverpool: The infamous Kop now houses an exciting array of executive boxes, many fitted with screens so you don't even have to watch the game! Capacity: 20,000. Admission: 12-seat box £850, 8-seat box £560, seats £30.

Manchester United: Moved to the magnificent G-Mex Stadium in 1998 after amalgamating with neighbours City and Oldham. The stadium holds as many as 6,000 in luxurious boxes, offers superb catering and houses both the delightful Manchester Heritage Theme Park and the Bobby Charlton Memorial Hairdressing Salon. Admission: 12-seat box £850, 8-seat box £560, 6-seat family box £300.

North East United: Despite some of the best facilities in the country, NEU has suffered financially due in the main to a well-organised boycott by former supporters of Newcastle, Sunderland and Middlesbrough. Millionaire Chief Executive 'Wor' Mirandinha has reputedly ploughed some £15 million into the club he claims to have loved since childhood. Capacity: 12,000. Admission: 12-seat box £650, 8-seat box £400, seat £30.

Nottingham/Derby: Sir Robert Maxwell's plaything, this club offers perhaps the best business facilities in the country with a comfortable all-boxed, 5000 capacity stadium. Admission: 12-seat box £700, 8-seat box £480, 6-seat family box £300.

Tottenham: Irving Scholar, founder of the first all-boxed stadium in 1994, still offers a remarkably comfortable stay in

Chelsea Independent

WIMBLEDON, 1-3, SOMEWHERE NEAR IBIZA, FEB 18TH. WELL, ACTUALLY NEAR JAVEA, BUT IT DOESN'T RHYME WITH ETHER

I sat in the shade of a big orange tree
And I fiddled once more with my knob
For it can be a pain, the terrain down in Spain
When you're one of the World Service mob
Who every weekend, all far flung and wide
Are poking their wires to the ether
To hear that their favourites have been stuffed again
In Irkutsk, Iran and Ibiza

I knew that an hour or so had gone by
So I tried again on my tranny
Where I heard Peter Jones say in crackling tones
That *"Grimsby are really uncanny!"*
So I thought bugger me! Could it be
That we've scored or we're drawing or stuffing the mooners?
Let's show them our arses, for our own catharthis
Is not going to be wooden spooners

But sad to relate, like poor Terry Waite
Our bicycle rusts in the rain
Of fame and good fortune we've eaten our portion
The bread and butter remain
I write with a frown that we're out but not down
And I knew as I sat by that tree
That the Muse says you'll lose if you only score one
And the bastards in blue have scored three.

PHIL BALL

the superb Scholar Stadium with its staggering 20,000 capacity. During the close season the arena plays host to a number of Hummel-sponsored fashion previews presented by roly-poly entrepreneur and chocolate factory owner Sir Gazza Gascoigne. Admission: 12-seat box £1000, 8-seat box £640, 6-seat family box £360.

West London Utd: Emerged in 1996 with the decline of Chelsea, Fulham, QPR, Wimbledon, Crystal Palace and Brentford. True to its surroundings, this ground offers you all the razzamatazz of the West End. Excellent cocktail and wine bars, superb hotel accomodation in a fashionable part of London. A must-see is the Patrick Nevin Memorial Record Library, which includes the tiny Cocteau Twins sound archive. Capacity: 20,000. Admission: 12-seat box £900 8-seat box £600, Seat £30.

Yorkshire County: Formed in 1999 with the amalgamation of North and South Yorkshire FCs, the Sheffield club is the League's youngster. County play at Hillsborough, leaving Leeds United to move back to Elland Road (former home of North Yorkshire FC) where they play in the GM Vauxhall Conference. Best of the amazing facilities is the welcoming hostelry *The Professional Yorkshireman* where the juke box plays soundtracks from Hovis adverts. Capacity, 12,000. Admission: 12-seat box £800, 8-seat box £520, Seat £25.

BRADFORD PARK AVENUE FOOTBALL CLUB

1/-

OFFICIAL PROGRAMME

Introduction

Bradford Park Avenue F.C. will always have a special place in my affections. I grew up in Huddersfield in the 1960's and like most football-daft lads supported the local team, but there were two other teams I tried to get to watch if 'Town' were playing miles away. One was Manchester City, who first impressed me when they came to Huddersfield in 1965-6 and swelled the growd to 32,000 with thousands of good-natured fans who changed ends at half-time by walking across the pitch en masse!

This would be the club I would come to support regularly when I started to live in the area years later. The other was Bradford Park Avenue, only a short bus ride away and then a brisk walk from the centre of Bradford. "Avenue" were the perrenial whipping boys of the Fourth Division, finishing next-to-bottom in 1966-67 and bottom in the next three years. I don't recall actually ever seeing them win when I went to see them but there was something about the ground with its "Dolls House" pavilion in the corner, and something about the dogged and self-deprecating supporters which made the club special to me; I looked for their results and groaned inwardly most Saturday tea-times when yet another defeat was broadcast.

Significant

When I went to see Bradford Park Avenue v Scunthorpe on April 4th 1970, I didn't realise how significant that game would be. It wasn't that Avenue lost 0-5, or even that a young lad playing for Scunthorpe called Keegan scored twice, it was that this would prove to be the last home game played in the Football League for the club lost their re-election campaign and Cambridge were voted in. From then on it was downhill all the way, the club went into the Northern Premier League and in 1974 went into voluntary liquidation. That seemed to be that.

Re-birth

Then one day late last year I read a piece in a publication called "Programme Monthly" that Bradford Park Avenue had been re-formed and were playing in the West Riding County Amateur Football League Division 3 in 1988-89.

A group of loyal supporters, including some who had kept a Sunday team going since the collapse of 1974, had got together and held a public meeting to generate enthusiasm. They had got a share of a ground next to Manningham Mills Cricket ground, entry into a League and sponsorship for a kit of green and white (the colours Avenue wore when they once graced the First Division). Rarely had an article left me more enthusiastic and I determined to go over to see the new set-up. Finally an opportunity arose in February; City were at Portsmouth, the shopping had been done and the kids were bored. This was it- the promise of a fish and chip lunch at a cafe on the way, quelled the dissenters and "Avenue" could look forward to four itinerants swelling their gate.

Skipping a beat

My heart always skips a beat when I approach a football ground and I wasn't disappointed to see two lads wearing scarves reminiscent of "Avenue" scarves of the '60's blocking the entry to the mecca behind the cricket club wall. £1.50 and we were all in. Would I like a programme? Would I? I shoved the 50p in his hand before he'd finished his sentence. A programme is a great memento and since I hadn't bought an "Avenue" programme for almost 19 years, I thought it was about time I forked out! The setting of the ground was magnificent, overlooking the city of Bradford on a windswept hill, with a small wooden stand on one side and Cricket Ground on the other. A clubhouse served tea and pies and peas and most enjoyably I met up with a couple of guys I know from my programme-collecting life, which led to various reminiscences.

The game

The game itself against Savile Arms was a 5-4 thriller complete with two own goals and a controversial penalty. None of your midfield-dominated football and blanket defence - both teams wanted to score as many goals as possible and at last I'd seen 'Avenue' win. My daughter Shirley reported that a close inspection of the crowd revealed an attendance of 60 (including two babies in push-chairs and the reserves) and two dogs. This was a million miles away from I.D.Cards and a million miles from the 80,000 crowd which saw "Avenue" draw 1-1 with Manchester United at Maine Road in the F.A Cup in 1949, which the programme referred to, but it was grass-roots football inspired by real enthusiasts at its best. Up the 'Avenue!

Tony Grayson

GREAT STUFF!

GLOOM

WELL, IT'S A DAY OUT, I SUPPOSE

King of the Kippax

THE COP END

Where am I???

Taking The Biscuit

1. One Tuesday in November I attended a football match in London. I found the ground without too much difficulty, wandered around for a bit, and then started waiting for the editor of this esteemed publication to arrive so I could dump my holdall in his car. Fifteen minutes before the kick off he still hadn't turned up so I decided to get inside the ground before the "Rush".

Once inside I was met by a line of police, searching all and sundry for the weapons that they know we all carry with us. "Open the bag" I was told (The days of "Please" and "Thank you" have long since gone.)

Once I had done this the man in blue proceeded to pull both sides apart as far as possible. As the sound of tearing reached my ears I helpfully pointed out that he was in fact ripping up the stitching. This fell on deaf ears, so I contented myself with dreaming up headlines such as "P.C. in wanton vandalism, shock horror probe." However my reverie was interrupted as the man found my flag and said "What flag is this?" ("London coppers ARE stupid – Exclusive"). So I told him what a union jack was.

The fairly major hurdle of getting past the thin (or should that be thick?) blue line was now over and I took up my spot on the terracing. The more vocal element of the crowd started up one of the favourite chants, "It's nice to know you're here, etc etc", at the pitiful gatherings of home supporters. This, however, ends in one of those four letter words which is perfectly acceptable on Channel 4, BBC 1, in newspapers, on records, is to be found in dictionaries and hear frequently in pubs, schools, shopping precincts but is considered indecent when uttered in football grounds.

The police response was immediate. "Any more of that and we'll nick the lot of you, starting with the ones on this side, so if you people (addressed to those of us on the side) want to see the game, you'd better make sure they keep quiet." This refers to one of those laws of the realm that were not debated in Parliament, do not appear on statute books, are denied existence of by police, politicians and journalists but which all football fans (and probably other groups such as ethnic minorities) know well, namely "It is an offence to stand next to a policeman when someone nearby, but too far away, commits a minor misdemeanour."

Not surprisingly the atmosphere became rather muted after that, with no-one giving even the slightest excuse for being ejected. Attempts to strike up any kind of witty repartee with the police were met with by stony stares, smiling no doubt being another criminal offence of the future (watch out Glasgow). I didn't see anyone ejected just before half time when the heinous crime of "Standing in a gangway" met with the only possible reply (personally, I think hanging is too good for such villains).

During the second half there was a steady procession of supporters, each with two policemen, out of the ground. Most seemed to be for uttering one swear word in the heat of the moment, although one lad in front of me appeared a trifle unlucky to suffer for "putting his right arm in the air. I'm told there were about 40 arrests. I wonder how many were charged after the game, let alone found guilty.

Basically, what should have been an enjoyable evening out was ruined by the actions in the "mindless majority" of the Metropolitan police force. Reading fans have no reputation of causing trouble over the last few years and the polices' action only served to alienate them from the supporters, in fact, if there had of been any trouble after the game, I think the police would have been partly held to blame.

One Tuesday in December I went to another football match in the same area of London, policed by the same authority as in match number 1. Also it has to be noted that the crowd were mostly male, entirely white and many were clearly the worse for alcohol.

Whilst being herded out of the station I heard singing which one month earlier would have been deemed offensive. The police did nothing. When I arrived at the stadium I realised that I didn't know where to go, so I asked a policeman for directions (Normally I don't do this as a matter of principal but in this case I wasn't sure that I would get a coherent answer from anyone else). The policeman was courteous, told me exactly where I wanted to go and even called me "Sir". Well actually the knighthood hasn't been announced yet... or could it be that he was being polite?

I got into the ground, past a large sign saying "NO BOTTLES OR CANS ALLOWED IN", and sat down next to a man swigging from a gin bottle.

There were quite a lot of police inside the ground but they only seemed interested in watching the game. When people swore they did nothing. When people walked onto the edge of the pitch so they could get tot the tea bar they did nothing. When a bottle was thrown onto the pitch in the second half they did nothing. In fact they made no attempt at all to antagonise fans – even to the extent of allowing bottles and cans to be used for their correct purposes, despite all the warnings posted around the ground.

At the end of the match there was a large scale pitch invasion. Except for keeping the entrance to the tunnel free, the police did nothing. While a large number of fans were standing on the pitch chanting and throwing seat cushions at each other, I took the opportunity to wander onto the pitch to view the stands from an angle supporters don't normally get a chance to see, and to try and imagine how it feels to have 50,000 people cheering you on. I narrowly avoided being hit by low flying cushions, but did manage to observe three people urinating on the pitch and one supporter attempting to carve up a foot square piece of turf. Yet again the custodians of law and order did nothing.

On the way back to the railway station I decided to ask for more directions, just to see how I was treated. Again the reply I received was courteous, the directions precise and accurate, and the word "Sir" was again used to address me. It's almost enough to restore ones faith.

Most Reading supporters reading this will recognise the first match as the away game this year at Fulham, although the general picture could have just as easily have been Crystal Palace, Grimsby or Bournemouth in 1987: or various home games in '85 and '86. The second match was in fact a rugby football match – the Varsity game between Oxford and Cambridge which I attended in an attempt to relive my student days. (As it was I ended up, I was just left wondering what it was I ever saw in female students).

There are two questions to be asked

(A) Why do the police feel the need to intimidate Association Football supporters.

(B) If the police are determined to take no action at a Rugby match then why do so many of them need to be there?.

The answer to the second one is probably something to do with the occasion – matches at Twickenham are the places to be at, as all the sponsors will testify, but if the police are going to take no action, I'm sure there are better things they could be doing. Returning to the issue of football matches, there is no real need for police to intimidate Reading fans – examples of excellent police forces were those in Shrewsbury and Plymouth who will strike up conversations with fans, provide assistance where necessary and generally behave in a decent and humane manor.

Looking back it seems the treatment of away fans is worse at larger clubs. Is this because the police think "Ah ha, little Reading, soft touch. Let's assert our authority". The Chief constable of the west midlands admitted to a branch of the Football Supporters Association that intimidation of away fans was part of his force's tactics. This may or may not work in the short term but the cost is another group of people who feel antagonistic towards the police.

Bear in mind that if Moynihan gets his way with ID cards next season it is probable that you will lose your card if you are ejected from a ground. This means that you could be banned from all professional football matches simply for standing in a gangway, raising your arm, standing next to a policeman or just being in the wrong place at the wrong time.

NEW SIGNING FOR LIONS

NEW SIGNING

The feeling of discontent that has drifted around The Den about the left back position all season, has finally been quashed, by the signing of a new defender.

Nicky Coleman need not worry about first team football anymore, because the arrival of tough tackling John Stalker from Manchester has proven John Docherty's thirst for success. Stalker was first spotted in the Manchester League, an average player until, James Anderton's arrival, his new partner in defence. They both played together for several years, when John decided to further his career by playing abroad. His Manchester side made him assistant manager in an attempt to disuade him from leaving, this did not deter him however and he went to Ireland on loan, where he became an attacking full back with a shoot on sight policy in front of goal.

Stalker was soon to return to Manchester however after his relationship with management turned sour. Like so many players who go abroad Stalker's career had taken a turn for the worse, and after management suddenly lost confidence in him, he was to leave Manchester for good.

Stalker was then to try his hand at five-a-side football. He played in the prestigious 'Soap' league, for Brookside, competing against stars like Wicksy and Seth Armstrong.

February 1988 comes and Stalker signs for the mighty Lions.

STOP PRESS: We have just been informed that John Stalker is not a footballer at all, but a Policeman. Well this shines a completely new light on the matter. Um... This means we've got the report completely wrong, well... that's a bloody waste of money isn't it, we want half a new team not a bloody copper! What on earth have we bought him for ? Perhaps he's been signed to solve the mystery of the fifth floodlight? or the use of that infernal ribbon that's forced me to vacate my very own personal barrier? or perhaps he will find out why George Lawrence has taken so long to recover? or even why there has been a plastic bag attached to a light on top of the stand for years? Personally I think John Stalker will be more use with a pair of football boots on.

The Lion Roars

I'VE BEEN REFEREEING FOOTBALL FOR TWENTY YEARS, SON, AND THAT WAS **WELL** OFFSIDE.

STRANRAER, around 1982

The last issue of AWOL was more than a bit harsh on our friends in blue - not without reason. But not all cops are out to arrest their way to a set of stripes - many are good-humoured and long-suffering and just dying to get back to their houses for Brookside.

JESUS CHRIST... HOW DO THOSE CLOWNS EVER HOPE TO BE TAKEN SERIOUSLY?

PUGH PUGH BARNEY McGREW

DUMBARTON, 1985-ish

EXCUSE ME, OFFICER, WHERE'S THE NEAREST PUB?

PAST THE STAND, TURN LEFT, DOWN THE HILL AND OVER THE CROSSROADS. IT'S ABOUT A HUNDRED YARDS ON ... IT'S CALLED "G.J.'s", A GREAT PINT.

DUNDEE, the 3-0 cup tie

COME ON THISTLE GET INTAE THIS SHI.... AHEM.

K A BIG MEDGE

PC Murdoch at BRECHIN

I'M NO' WATCHIN' ANY TEAM THAT GETS BEAT BY F...ING MEADOW-BANK!

NAB

AYE YOU ARE, SON... FOUL LANGUAGE, YOU'RE STAYING TILL **FULL TIME**.

TYNECASTLE, Shield destruction, 1978?

I CAN'T DRAW HANDS. SOREY.

APOLOGISE!

GALA casual wank, 1986

WHITE SOCKS

AYE, THERE'S A FEW WILD BOYS HERE... BUT THERE'S NOTHING TO WORRY ABOUT

SNARL

Not bloody much. Early days at BERWICK

The cops at East Fife, Dunfermline, Aberdeen and Stirling all could have got mentions, while the policing at Falkirk seems to have improved, going by the Skol Cup tie; but the Hamilton mob may be efficient but are boorish and arrest-happy, the Dumfries police are like the Hamilton force without the efficiency or the arrests, and if when I am cremated some of the smoke drifts north of Aviemore it will still be too soon to get close to those casuals in uniform that masquerade as the Inverness police force.

WE'LL GIVE YOU AN ESCORT OUT OF TOWN, JUST IN CASE THERE'S ANY TROUBLE.

STATION PARK

IN FORFAR?

HE MEANS WELL

AM.

Start of this season. The last recorded trouble at Station Park was in 1896 when someone farted at a charabanc.

THE BOOK OF FOOTBALL QUOTATIONS

KIRKCALDY

When you come to a place like ~~Barcelona~~ you think 'Bloody Hell, I wish I was back in England.'

RANGERS 1989

TERRY BUTCHER, ~~Ipswich defender, 1979~~.

The Wild Rover

KENT.— Beckenham 0; Whitstable 0; Crockenhill 0; Met Police 0; Danson 0; Tunbridge Wells 0; Darenth 0; Chatham 0; Deal 0; Thames Poly 0; Faversham 0; Greenwich 0; Herne Bay 0; Cray 0; Hythe 0; Alma Swanley 0; Kent Pol 0; Slade Green 0; Sittingbourne 0; Ramsgate 0.

from The People -
28th August 1988

Frank Large

It appears that the Third Division may not after all be the last bastion of attacking football. A glance at the results in the Winstonlead Kent League Division One seems to suggest that the 'garden of England' could well be a breeding ground for a new Frank Large or a budding Dean Coney.

There's Only One F in Fulham

The Weary Traveller

It has been my misfortune over the last three years or so, to have travelled regularly to Gills away games, and sample the culinary delights available to weary travellers who have forgotten to eat sufficiently at the service station on the way up (that stuff is not much better either). Here are a few examples of what Keith Floyd may not have included in his series on UK cuisine.

Cardiff City March 1986:-

You can actually taste the domestos in the coffee here if left for 10 minutes can be served in slices.

Brentford April 1986, February 1987, April 1988:-

Tea unbelievably bad - worst in football league. Stagnant swamp water with tsetse fly topping. No taste - if tested by eminent scientists, will probably prove radioactive. Saturday October 1st produced the expected result, a cup of bubbling watered down sewage.

Chesterfield January 1986 & February 1988:-

Delighted to find on reaching front of queue that the pies were sold out, having had one on a previous visit. Questionable filling. Possibility of archeological finds if four pies bought as a job lot.

Kettering November 1986:-

Mention must be made here of the lavatorial facilities: three aluminium plastic symbols, self contained with complimentary bucket. The third such hut bore the word "Ladies" on the door. A brief glimpse inside showed the only difference to its two male use only counterparts was a wooden seat, attached to the bucket via dubious fittings. Keen observers would have noticed the tea urn being wheeled around the pitch at half time, concealing a vibrant, steaming brew. Strange that the buckets appeared empty in the second half.

—A. Mitchell

Brian Moore's Head

DON'T EVER LET THE DREAM FACTORIES DIE

1985/86-the make or break year, the year of clubs going to the wall, of the Super League, of the falling gates. For me, 1985/86 has been a season of revelation-revelation that amongst the talk of splits there lies a hidden side of football that had eluded me-the true gulf between the "big" clubs and the small. I've been to most of the London grounds this year and yet I've always left feeling cheated-cheated of the cosy inimacy, the grotty pie shack, the quirky ground, and the obvious passion of the die-hard local fans. When you visit Chesterfield, or Chester; Carlisle, or Cardiff; half the fun is the local flavour.

What the Super-Leaguers miss, because they simply can't recognise it, is this uniqueness that is present only in the provinces-a richness and flavour that even your Derbys and Sheffields have, but Spurs lost decades ago. For those who would see the League diminished I offer this observation. Football is the mass spectator sport that it is, at its week-in, week-out best, because it is an intimate game. The supporter united with fellow supporter and his team for 90 minutes each week. This spirit is born of regular acquaintance, it is the very basis of the attraction of the game on a freezing winter afternoon. Without that the game is unrecognisable, devoid of atmosphere to the true supporter.

In that way the same 20,000 or 2,000 may meet each week in a roar, a passion that is obvious to the visitor. Go to Loftus Road, White Hart Lane or Stamford Bridge and what hits you at once is the lack of warmth, of community. In these places football is a spectacle, to be taken up one week and dropped at a whim the next, on the level of a TV show, and here lies an obvious lesson. The Super-Leaguers would have us watching football as served up on the box-a casual acquaintance with teams, players, atmosphere, sanitised and at a safe distance.

Perversly this seems to me to offer great hope for the future of the local team. I follow Bristol, not Bradford, City, although friends have dragged me from Manchester to Southend to watch the Bantams. For all the "smaller" clubs the message must be the same-retain your tradition and identity at all costs, to meet the "giants" half way is to lose your most valuable asset. Clubs will ultimately survive not on the spectacle of the football played fortnightly, but on the commitment of their local followers. In hard times many have fought for the survival of Hull, Swansea, Derby, Bristol City and Bradford City-who, on the other hand would miss a fallen QPR or their like, stripped of identity, of all magic, marketed like soap and playing the game, with clinical precision, in a barren multi-purpose dome?

STEVE HOCKING

City Gent

Alternative Football for Fulham!

There's Only One F in Fulham

WHEN SUNDAY COMES
ISSUE 3   OCT 1988   40 PENCE

IAN WHO?

LIVERPOOL SIGN UNKNOWN WELSH DUSTMAN
INSIDE: Loads more out of date stuff

COOKALIKE

CRIKEY! THERE'S NO **ANSWER** TO THAT!

COOK   PENFOLD

Has anyone noticed the uncanny resemblance between Dundee supremo Angus Cook and 'Dangermouse' star Penfold ? Surely they must be related ?

Yours,

£500 Bet,
Broughty Ferry, Dundee

The Final Hurdle

Saturday Comes
FOOTBALL Magazine
March 1989 No. 25

THE PEOPLE

50p

Atkinson Bounces Back

You'll work in Spain one day, Ron

No, I'll be there for at least a fortnight

KITS

Are you the next Pierré Cardin?

Yes, its your chance to design the new WEST HAM KIT

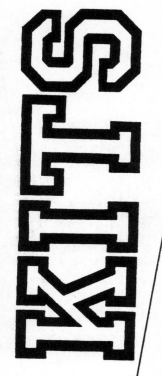

↑ COULD THIS BE WEST HAM'S KIT FOR 89/90

West Ham are soon to take the field in yet another new strip.

Could YOU be the one to design it for us?

To test your suitability, first answer these three simple questions.

1. Have you ever designed West ham's kit before

2. Do you know anything about the traditional colours & design of West ham's kit?

3. Do you care what the end product looks like as long as it makes money.?

If your answer to all three questions was 'no', then you could be the one for the job. Designing the football kit of the 80's opens up a whole world of possibilities. One only has to look at Man.city (red & black check squares) Portsmouth, (Salmon pink) & Sheffield Weds. (grey & mauve!), to see what can be done to away kits.

But why stop there, Traditional 'Home' colours also need changing, & Southampton's streaky bacon-style 'Danish' look has been all the rage on the south coast this year!

Remember, you can make whatever changes you feel necessary, though we'd prefer claret & blue to be included somewhere in the design.

THE GOOD OLD DAYS

← SPOT THE DIFFERENCE →

ASTON VILLA

SOUTHAMPTON

The Boleyn Scorcher

Send your new designs to the Boleyn Scorcher straght away, remember the sooner we recieve them the sooner we can market them to all those eager 10-year olds (and their parents of course) * As a special bonus to the winner the winning design will be modell... ...se stars of the clothes show ...... & ...... hire.

****
Another thing sure to get you banging your head against the wall in frustration is the club's attitude towards our away kit. Every bloody year, fans write in and say why did we wear yellow for such and such a match? Why can't we play in red and change our shorts or socks. These letters are printed on the programme page. And what is the response from Arsenal?.....
● What do other supporters think?
Tim Johnson, in the Luton programme, says, "Why can't the team be provided with red shorts, so that at away matches e.g. Everton, Millwall, QPR, we can retain our red?" Arsenal's reply......
● What do other supporters think?
"Dear Adolf Hitler, why oh why do you keep killing thousands of innocent people right across Europe?"
Adolf replies.....
● What do other supporters think?
********************** * Arsenal Echo Echo

Senorés,

AN APOLOGY TO RON ATKINSON

We feel very sorry for Ron Atkinson. We feel even sorrier for Sheffield Wednesday. It's been a sad do, Ron Ron.

Jesus Gil
President, Atletico Madrid

Just Another Wednesday

KITS

After 6 issues of The Ugly Inside it's about time we mentioned SICK, no not the feeling you get after watching Saints play and not even the thick yellow gooey substance that can be found sticking your face to the pillow on Sunday morning after a particularly heavy night on the Town. No we mean SICK, the new campaign for Saints In Conventional Kit (clever eh!). As mentioned in the last issue it's about time Saints returned to the famous old Red and White Stripes, and after talking to many Saints fans this would seem to be the popular choice. In recent years weve seen our beloved team stroll up and down the country in at what can best be described as cast offs for Star Trek, (Patrick & then Hummell) so we are now left with Danish Pyjama Jackets. However, with the new subtle shadow designs and fashionable collars (eg England) surely it wouldn't be too hard to include these modern features on a traditional Red and White striped shirt. Also why on earth after victory at Wembley did Saints ever change their away kit. Well here at U.I. HQ we have a theory on that one. At the time big Lawrie's daughter was just starting secondary education at St Annes, so it was no suprise when Saints changed their away kit to the same school colours as St Annes. Ever since then weve had to put up with a poxey away kit although the all White strip doesent look so bad! Red and White and Yellow and Blue should be the order of the day so come on all you SICK minded people, why not write into us or better still write to The Dell to Show that we want The Stripes!

Saints are back in stripes...

Back to Admiral whose shirts must have been some of the most uncomfortable garments ever made. Now come on admit it. we all bought a couple of those £5 cheap Wolves, Leeds, or American team shirts from THE GOALPOST and found you couldnt wear them for fear of losing half your skin, ripped off by the fibre-glass material. THe Franciscan monks' hairshirts had nothing on these. I bought a Los Angeles Aztecs one myself, but some of my friends had Detroit Express, and Chicago Sting among others.

The introduction of Adidas into the British market did a lot to raise the standard of the British football shirt. Their shiny, silky made for Birmingham, Ipswich and Dundee Utd originally seemed to make the others have a closer look at their product. There then followed the introduction of the pin stripe, the button collar, the V-neck colour and various other money spinning alternatives.

The present day trend seems to be to try and create a shirt which the average bed could wear to the Friday night disco without feeling out of place. The prime ers are the hideous Scotland second strip which looks like a pyjama top, and that bloody Celtic away top which even has the "runaway criminals" arrows on it...are they trying to say something ?

I think the fact that the design of the shirt didnt change basically for 70 or so years shows what a disgraceful cash in the trend of today is. Change it every couple of years so the hard pushed parent has to buy a new one to save the boy being out of dates with his mates. Its time they played fair and gave a new strip at least 5 years life before changing it.

Others worth a mention: present St Mirren bib design
Huddersfield away strip (same as St Mirren) but a green and yellow colour
Man City black and red squares away kit
Hibs purple second strip
Clydebanks wavey lines

AWOL

COURAGE COURAGE COURAGE COURAGE COURAGE COURAGE COURAGE READING F.C.

Artists Impression of new Reading pendant, with sponsors name subtly introduced.

Taking The Biscuit

SCOTLAND IN COURT
JESTER TRACKSUIT
SENSATION

Dateline........Jan 31st 1989. Umbro HQ Milan. Informed sources continue to report that rumours still flourish about the Scotland strip,the change strip and the medieval jester's outfit having been designed by the YTS kid as a result of a 1000lire bet with his pals.Meanwhile, Public Relations at Umbro continue to deny the recent allegation that Gina the cleaner designed the Aberdeen strip and the change strip while she was doing the hoovering.

THIS WILL BE A REALLY TOUGH ONE ARCHIE'

Yes - Scotland have bought the strip!

Andy Roxburgh in the new Scotland tracksuit.

The Northern Light

And finally..!

This particular contributor is sick to the proverbial back teeth of hearing of K.F.C.'s 'Glory Years'; of Jimmy Broon and Frank Beattie; of Real Madrid and Eintracht Frankfurt. However when an uncle recently reassured me that Killie would be back, it set me thinking -- in 30 years time when Killie are the scourge of Europe, what tales of the current years can I relate to my fanatic relations? I can just see it now ......

"Oh yes. Well, you see in them days, we had <u>room</u> at Rugby Park. None of this 35,000 nonsense. We could communicate more easily with the players. Especially Stuart McLean. And then of course there were the away games. See your generation, they don't get to go to <u>real</u> football grounds. Yer stadium of Light and yer Bernabau, that's no <u>real</u> football. I'm talking about Links Park and Bayview and Shawfield. That's where <u>real</u> football is played. None of yer poncy seven figure signing on fees and civic receptions. That's all artificial. That's not what football is all about.

D'ye know, I can mind going to Glebe Park on a Tuesday night -- a hundred of us there were. I can mind when Killie lost to teams like St Johnstone, Forfar and even Ayr United. Aye, and they even lost to Inverness Thistle and Auchinleck Talbot. What's that? -- you canny believe that? Neither could we ...... Ach, but we were happy in them days. We had nothing to live up to so we weren't disappointed. I can even remember the day we snatched a last minute equaliser in the third round of the Scottish Cup away to Queen of the South. Oh yes, I wouldnae swop places wi'ye even if I could ......"

Paper Roses

A-Z FANZINES

CLUB-BASED

Aberdeen
The Northern Light
Airdrieonians
Only The Lonely
Albion Rovers
Over the Wall
Aldershot
Shots In The Dark
Arsenal
An Imperfect Match
Arsenal Echo Echo
The Gooner
One-Nil Down, Two-One Up
Aston Villa
Witton Wisdom
Auchinleck Talbot
Three In A Row
Ayr United
4-1
Barnet
Buzztalk
Where's The Number On Your Back?
Birmingham City
Tired and Weary
Bishop's Stortford
Cross Rhodes
Blackpool
The Basil
Bolton Wanderers
Normid Nomad
Wanderers Worldwide
Boston United
From Behind Your Fences
Bournemouth
NotTheEightthousandandfivehundredandtwo
Out Of Court
Bradford City
City Gent
Bernard of the Bantams (comic)

Brentford
Voice of the Beehive
Brighton & Hove Albion
And Smith Must Score!
Gull's Eye
Bristol City
The Bountyhunter
Bristol Rovers
The Gashead
Bromley
Down The Lane
Burton Albion
Up Front
Cambridge United
The Abbey Rabbit
Cardiff City
Bluebird of Happiness
Bobbing Along
Intifada
Watch The Bluebirds Fly
Celtic
Not The View
Charlton Athletic
Addikted
Lennie Lawrence
Voice of the Valley
Chelsea
Chelsea Independent
The Red Card
Cheltenham Town
Murphy's Frog
Chesterfield
The Crooked Spireite
Cliftonville
The Wee Red
Clydebank
Le Chic
Alternative Kilbowie Comment
Colchester United
Floodlight
Coventry City
The West Ender

Crewe Alexandra
He's Not Danny Grady
Crystal Palace
Eagle Eye
Darlington
Mission Impossible/Terminated
Dartford
Light At The End Of The Tunnel
Dulwich Hamlet
Champion Hill Street Blues
Dundee
Derry Rumba
Dundee United
The Final Hurdle
Freakscene
One Team In Dundee
Dundee Utd/West Ham
UTD United
Dunfermline Athletic
Walking Down The Halbeath Road
East Kilbride Thistle
Jag Mag
Emfa (Kilkenny)
Every Man A Football Artist
Enfield
In Defence
Talk of the Town End
Everton
Blue Wail
When Skies Are Grey
Exeter City
The Exe-Directory
Falkirk
Falkirk Unofficial Fanzine
Fulham
There's Only One F in Fulham
Gillingham
Brian Moore's Head
Capital Gills
Grimsby Town
Sing When We're Fishing
Harwich & Parkeston
Shrimpers Review
Heart of Midlothian
Heartbeat
The Good, the Bad and the Ugly
Hibernian
Down the Slope
North-east Hibernian
The Proclaimer
Hi-bees Glasgow Gossip
Hibs Monthly
Hull City
Hull, Hell and Happiness
Ipswich Town
A Load Of Cobbolds
Dribble
Kidderminster Harriers
The Soup
Kilmarnock
Killie Ken
Paper Roses
Kingstonian
NHS
Leeds United
Crossbar

The Hanging Sheep
Marching Altogether (Anti-racist)
The Peacock
Leicester City
The Fox
Leyton Orient
Leyton Orientear
Lincoln City
The Banker Magazine
Linfield
Blue For You
One Team In Ulster
Liverpool
When Sunday Comes
Macclesfield Town
Silk Yarns
Manchester City
Electric Blue
Blue Print
King of the Kippax
Manchester United
Red Issue
Red News
Mansfield Town
Size 10½ Boots
Meadowbank Thistle
AWOL
The Thitsle
Middlesbrough
Ayresome Angel
Fly Me To The Moon
Millwall
The Lion Roars
Montrose
Mo Mo Super Mo
Morton
The Cappielow Bugle
Newcastle United
Jim's Bald Head
The Mag
Northampton Town
What A Load Of Cobblers
Northwich Victoria
Resign Roberts, Re-sign
Who's He On Loan From?
Norwich City
The Citizen
Never Mind The Danger
Nottingham Forest
Brian
Notts County
The Pie
Nottm Forest/Notts County
400 Yards
Oxford United
Raging Bull
Peterborough United
The Peterborough Effect
Portsmouth
The Greatest City
Port Vale
The Memoirs of Seth Bottomley
The Wright's Pie
Preston North End
The PNE View
Queen's Park
The Web

Queen's Park Rangers
A Kick Up The Rs
In The Loft
Raith Rovers
The Wild Rover
Rangers
Aye Ready
Follow, Follow
Reading
Elm Park Disease
Taking The Biscuit
St Johnstone
Wendy Who?
St Mirren
There's A Store Where The Creatures Meet
Love Street Syndrome
Shamrock Rovers
Glenmalure Gazette
Sheffield United
Flashing Blade
Sheffield Wednesday
Just Another Wednesday
Southampton
The Ugly Inside
Southend United
The Seasider
True Blues Magazine
Stirling Albion
The Beanos
Stoke City
All Stoked Up
The Jolly Potter
The Oatcake
Sunderland
Wise Men Say

Swansea City
Jackmail
Swindon Town
Bring The Noise
Tooting & Mitcham
Occasional Terrorist
Tooting Tearaways
Torquay United
Mission Impossible
Tottenham Hotspur
The Spur
Tranmere Rovers
Friday Night Fever
Waterlooville
Foul
Watford
Mud, Sweat and Beers
Wealdstone
The Elmslie Ender
West Bromwich Albion
Fingerpost
West Ham United
The Boleyn Scorcher
Fortune's Always Hiding
Never Mind The Boleyn
On The Terraces
Wigan Athletic
The Cockney Latic
Wimbledon
Yidaho!
Witton Albion
Bishop 3-1
Wycombe Wanderers
Chairboys Gas
Yeovil Town
Huish Roar
York City
Terrace Talk

GENERAL
The Absolute Game (Scotland)
Balls!
Crazy Horse
Elfmeter (West Germany)
European Football
Five To Three
Football and Fiesta! (Europe)
Head The Ball (Ireland)
Hit The Bar (North-west)
The Lad Done Brilliant (Humour)
Les Bence – Manager's Notes (Humour)
Libero (Italy)
A Lotta Balls (Scotland)
More Than A Game
Non-League Football Fanfare
Off The Ball (RIP)
Punt (Scotland)
Pyramid (Non-League)
Reclaim The Game (FSA)
Rodney, Rodney
Scottish Non-League Review
Sound Of The Crowd (Scotland)
Storming With Menace (South-west/Lager)
Tayside Football Review
This Way Up
When Saturday Comes
* **WHEN SATURDAY COMES** (monthly) lists addresses and prices of all fanzines. * **SPORTSPAGES** Bookshop, London and **FOOTBALL CRAZY**, Edinburgh, stock most of the above.

ACKNOWLEDGEMENTS

All fanzine editors and contributors, whether or not their efforts appear in this book, can take as read my gratitude and admiration. Their enthusiasm for the game has been an inspiration.

For material and encouragement I owe thanks to Laurie Alder, Stuart Basson, Stephen Borland, Adrian Brown, Richard Cairns, Paul Caulfield, Anthony Coffey, Chris Collins, Pete Collins, Allan Collis, Thomas Conroy, Mick Dickinson, Steve Dixon, Mark Dingwall, Gerry Dunbar, Tony Ella, John Ellis, Sandy Fenwick, Final Hurdlers Martin and Steve, Clive Foley, Chris Frean, Gary Galbraith, Stephen Gardner, Chris Gavin, Judith Gibbons, Martin Gordon, Merv Grist, Robin Halls, Jes Hamblett, Guy Havord, Gary "Skip" Hills, Mark Jensen, Jamie J., Peter Jones, Mark Kelly and Nick of the Railway Paddock, Mike Kelly, Dave Knight, Rob Ledgar, David Lloyd, Guy Loveday , Gordon Markey, Rob Marshall, Simon Matters, Andy Medcalf, Alick Milne, Mark Murphy, Fintan Murray, Stuart Mutler, David McGill, John MacNeil, Colin McPherson, Nick of Abercynon, Gary Oliver, Neil Palfreyman, Kevin Pamphilon, Keith Paulin, Pete of Leeds Fans United against Racism & Fascism, Jamie Pigott, Carl and Howard Prosser, Steve Rapport, Sudhir Rawal, Alex Rimmer, Rob of VOTB, Bernard Savage, David Shedden, Andrew J. Smelt, Peter Smith, Richard O. Smith, Jon Southgate, Tim Stevens, Matt Stone, Nick Stringer, William Telford, Dave Thomas, Ian Tilley, Rob Trent, Andy Vaughan, Dave Wallace, and all those whose signatures were illegible or whose offerings were anonymous.

I am indebted to the many friends and colleagues who offered support and ideas, especially Steve Bierley, Charles Burgess, Simon Kelner, Adam Scott and Adrian Thrills; my thanks also to Mike Alway, Bill Brewster, John Dewhirst (a true Gent), John Duncan, Andy Lyons, Rogan Taylor, and to John Peel, whose disinclination to act his age is an example to us all.

Finally, my love and gratitude to Julie, Ellie and Joe, who tolerated my late nights spent studying strange packages brought by the postman and the takeover of our home by hundreds of wonderful magazines with funny names.

Phil Shaw
August, 1989